# THE
# SIX
# DEMONS
# OF LOVE

BOOKS BY STEVE BERMAN

**Non-Fiction**
RELATIONSHIPS (with Vivien Weiss)

**Children's**
WHAT TO BE

**Travel**
THE NORTHEASTERN OUTDOORS
SOUTHERN NEW ENGLAND FOR FREE

**Screenplays**
CONEY ISLAND (with Stephen L. Forman)
FIRES (with Stephen L. Forman)

# STEVE BERMAN

# THE SIX DEMONS OF LOVE

**McGraw-Hill Book Company**
New York · St. Louis · San Francisco · Bogotá
Guatemala · Hamburg · Lisbon
Madrid · Mexico · Montreal
Panama · Paris · San Juan · São Paulo · Tokyo · Toronto

2 3 4 5 6 7 8 9 F G R F G R 8 7 6 5

ISBN 0-07-004915-7

LIBRARY OF CONGRESS CATALOGING IN PUBLICATION DATA

Berman, Steve.
The six demons of love.
1. Love—Psychological aspects.    2. Men—Psychology.
I. Title.
BF575.L8B44 1984      646.7′7′088041        83-24398
ISBN 0-07-004915-7

Book design by Grace Markman

To Vivien—whose love surprised me,
making me happier than I ever thought
I could be.

The Women's Movement has developed very powerful spokespeople for changing women's roles. But
men's experience is different and only when we share
our hurt and sensitivity, our gentleness and strength
will we truly understand ourselves and each other.

—Geof Morgan

Those who love the truth must seek love in marriage,
love without illusions.

—Albert Camus

# ACKNOWLEDGMENTS

M Y WIFE AND I, for the past eight years, have been sharing our relationship's emotional ups and downs with several close friends. These friends, in turn, have confided their own joys and difficulties.

Our animated probings—when all of us are struggling to figure out some kink in one of our relationships—have been invaluable experiences for me. This book owes much to these friends. Their honesty has allowed me to discover my own. I'd especially like to thank Stephen L. Forman, Carol Pope, David Kinsey, Abbie Fink, Pamela Mills-Forman, Benson Forman, Ivy Colbert, Jeff McQueen, Amy Kahn, Sig VanRaan, Perry Garfinkle, Marcy Klapper, Laury Binney, Michael Shandler, Nina Shandler, Rob Brandt, Joan Swerdlow Brandt, Carolyn Colby, Robin Karson, Bob Brody, Estelle Gorfine, Roberta Issler, Joe Goren, Cindy Chandler-Worth, and John Colby.

Faculty members at the University of Massachusetts Counseling Psychology Program gave generously and wisdomfully to me. Their insights, in particular those relating to family systems, are reflected in the pages of this book. I'd like to thank Dr. Evan Imber Coppersmith, Dr. William Mathews, and Dr. Jack Wideman. In addition, Dr. Don Banks, Dr. George Levinger, and Dr. Sheryl Reichman-Hruska read the manuscript many times, offering encouragement and editorial insight.

Staff members of the Northampton Area Mental Health Clinic, in Northampton, Massachusetts, afforded me glimpses into modern psychoanalytic/psychodynamic thinking. I'm especially grateful to Dr. Michael Karson and to Dr. Lorraine Yasinski for their time and intellectual stimulation.

Most of all, I'm indebted to the hundreds of men and women who allowed me to interview them about their romantic relationships. Confidentiality doesn't permit me to name them here. But I again want to thank each one of them. Their contribution to this book is inestimable.

# CONTENTS

# PROLOGUE

WHY ANOTHER BOOK about love relationships? Haven't we all read enough magazine articles promising increased communication between spouses, enough self-help books about marriage?

Because what we haven't read nearly enough about are the emotional struggles *men* need to face in the land of love. Women's magazines are weekly filled with helpful hints to wives and would-be wives about romantic relationships. The emotional obstacle course men must maneuver, though, as they attempt to create and sustain intimate relationships has been only meagerly mapped. This is a book, therefore, about the emotional obstacles men encounter on love's often confusing path.

Some of these obstacles or *demons,* as I call them, are most active when a man and a woman first meet. Others quickly intensify once the question of marriage arises. Still others activate only after a couple has married. But regardless of when each of these demons most acutely affects a couple, if a man can identify and befriend them, then his romantic relationships (and, later on, his marriage) can thrive. But if he chooses to ignore them, loving relationships with members of the opposite sex just won't be part of his journey through life. So this book is really a primer, a guidebook to help men steer some of the perplexing labyrinths of marriage and love.

Because I'm a man, I've naturally chosen to understand these demons from a male point of view. But I feel that much of the book's material relates to women as well. All these demons operate in women's lives. I wrote, too, about these demons from a male perspective because men, I'm convinced, are more out of touch with them, and, therefore, less able to deal with them gracefully.

\*    \*    \*

Besides hundreds of interviews conducted with men and women of all ages and all socioeconomic backgrounds, my own relationship with my wife was a rich source of many of my insights into the "dance of intimacy" and its attendant demons. To write a book about "men and love," therefore, and not to include my personal wrestlings with these demons would have been to write an incomplete book. So I've included lengthy accounts of my own battles with each of these demons throughout these pages.

By writing very personally about my own "love journey," as well as by presenting other men's romantic lives, I want to place these obstacles, these emotional struggles, into some larger perspective. Every man's love journey is menaced by these same demons; all that ever really varies in different men's lives is the degree of each demon's ferocity. This larger perspective, this knowledge that all men wrestle with these same demons, hopefully will help to make each man's individual struggles less painful.

This book was written with the passionate hope that someday women will have more skilled and more willing partners in their pursuit of deeper and more meaningful love relationships. So many women I've spoken with, and so many of my closest women friends have told me how incredibly hurt and disillusioned they've been by men. Out of ignorance, fear, and rage, men just too frequently have condemned women for being overly emotional, overly fragile, and overly concerned about their love lives. But it's time for men to start taking their romantic lives more seriously: time for men to start knowing, as Virginia Woolf said, that women have other functions in romantic relationships than to serve as mirrors for men, reflecting them at twice their actual size.

*The Six Demons of Love* is the story of my own and other men's attempts at befriending the common demons of love and marriage. It's a book about how men can be better mates and husbands. It's a book that I hope men will want to buy on their own. But if they don't, then maybe their wives and lovers will buy it for them, inconspicuously placing it on night tables and dressers.

# INTRODUCTION

**A**FTER INTERVIEWING psychiatrists, psychologists, and other mental health workers, and speaking with over 375 men and women, I began to notice certain recurring stumbling blocks that inevitably—in relationship after relationship—got in the way of love. These were recurring obstacles that prevented men from emotionally giving to women. These obstacles, these basic complications that all men encounter in the land of love are, again, the *stuff* of this book.

For all its emotional upheavals, for all its unhinging confusions, I saw that love—that seemingly formless process whereby two people develop a true caring for one another—is at least partially understandable. Specifically, the forming of an intimate and meaningful love relationship can be viewed as a series of six confrontations or six battles with six very stubborn emotional demons. And it's in the process of overcoming these six obstacles where true love is both forged and sustained.

These six demons or six emotional obstacles are what keep all of us from our more playful and loving selves. They're what prevent us from creating truly intimate relationships. And, as I said earlier, women suffer with them. But men are strangled and struck dumb by them.

It's been ascertained by social psychologists that when people are asked what they remember as the happiest time of their lives, they inevitably include the first years of a new relationship. "There is the joy," according to the sociologist Jessie Bernard, "of having found each other, the enhancement of self by interaction with the other; the glow of mutual appreciation. Disenchantment has not yet reached great depths, and the novelty of the new relationship casts a halo over everything."

These years naturally have their torments, their "demons," if you will. But there's a newness, a "blanket of love" during this period of a relationship that enables these inevitable demons to be dealt with. If these obstacles or these demons are acknowledged early on and dealt with during these first years of a relationship, then the chances of creating a healthy emotional foundation—one that will serve the relationship well for whatever difficult times lie ahead—will be maximized. But if these demons go unheeded, the likelihood of the relationship surviving life's vicissitudes will be seriously diminished.

\*   \*   \*

As a man meets and then falls in love with a woman, he'll invariably encounter these demons. These six demons are: The Extinction Demon (the fear men have of losing their independence in a close relationship); the Fusion Demon (what happens when men fall desperately in love); the Anger Demon; the Jealousy Demon; the Time Demon (the tendency in men to slowly but steadily lose interest in their love relationships); and the Lust Demon (a demon that haunts almost every monogamous couple).

These demons, or more precisely, how casually most men wrestle with them (and in some cases, simply deny them), are the cause of all the familiar complaints women have about men; complaints women have so openly been voicing these past ten years: *Men don't know how to communicate their emotions. Men are preoccupied with their careers, with money, or with power. Men aren't spontaneously giving. Men see us only as sexual objects, not as individuals.*

This "demon schemata," as a tool for making our love relationships more understandable (and, therefore, more navigable), is useful. But it's important to note that by making each of these demons a separate entity, I don't want to misrepresent their essentially inextricable nature. These demons all live in the same lair, and when they surface, it's usually as one entwined mass: They have tentacles and claws that are sometimes so fused it's impossible to tell them apart.

\*     \*     \*

Before I actually begin this exploration of the six most common obstacles to love, I want to say just a few words about marriage; specifically, about men and marriage. Most guidebooks, after all, begin with a description of their destination.

According to David and Leslie Newman, the screenwriters of *Superman II*, Superman couldn't be married and remain Superman. Superman could either marry Lois Lane but then have to lose his "superman-ness" in the process; or he could remain Superman but thereby have to forfeit the comforts of married life.

Being Superman *and* being married just wasn't possible.

Heroes and marriages obviously don't mix very well in our pop culture. Our television heroes are usually young cops, each with a stable of attractive but expendable girlfriends. Fighting crime—and not exploring the intricacies of romantic relationships—is their lives' greatest passion: handsome, unmarried workaholics

who'd really rather pursue a heroin ring than a marriage ring.

Being married, then, is antiheroic in our society. For
a man to really be a man, we're subliminally told, he
can't be limited by the humdrum intimacy of married
life. And this isn't only a prejudice held by men. I've
heard many women bemoan the fact that someone as
dynamic, say, as Paul Newman is happily married. They
feel cheated somehow, as if so sexy and successful a man
shouldn't be taken out of commission by the inevitable
restraints of marriage.

Clearly, marriage is antiheroic for men in our culture.
Cooking a dinner for his wife, sharing his deepest jeal-
ousies, or trying to resolve a knotty problem about his
kid's schooling are all superfluous to our modern heroes. Heroes aren't to be mired in too much of that sort
of mundane muck. There are other, more important
feats for them to perform.

Given these societal prejudices, it didn't surprise me
that most men, when I asked them to assess the suc-
cesses and failures of their lives, either skipped over or,
at best, paid a glib and self-conscious attention to their
marriages. Careers, children, net worth, a cabin they
built ten years ago with their own hands all took prece-
dence in their self-evaluations.

Despite all the media hype these past fifteen years
about the "Me" generation and its intensive emotional
explorations, I found that most men in our society are
still reluctant to talk or to write about their romantic
relationships or their marriages. It's rarely the focus of
their sharpest faculties. Indeed, brilliant, accomplished
men often ended up having the sophistication of four-
teen-year-olds when finally coaxed into talking about

their relationships or marriages. Exactly what it means to be a good husband, therefore, is something nobody really talks about anymore: If you describe somebody nowadays as being a "good husband," chances are you're dismissing them as being either plodding or unexciting.

*    *    *

This reluctance among men to reflect upon their love relationships has been exacerbated in recent years by the fact that a new criterion is being formulated by women for what constitutes a good husband or mate: In the past twenty years, women have made a successful assault on the job market. They've gotten hold of some of the reins of power. As a result, they're now looking much less to marriage and men for financial support. Marriage has shifted, as the psychiatrist Carol Nadelson points out, ". . . from an emphasis on survival and economic security to a focus on companionship, love, and communication. Self-fulfillment is a value that has superseded the more traditional concerns about family loyalties and responsibilities."

Women now want men to be more than mere wage earners. They want them to be their emotional companions. But men, unfortunately, have always been (and remain) quiet enemies of emotions, both their own and their wives'.

If there was one recurring theme in all the interviews I conducted with women, it was their need, expressed in almost identical terms, for their lovers and husbands to be more expressive, more tender, more emotional. *Noncommunicative, quiet, hostile, superficial* were adjectives I consistently heard women using to describe their men. Men need to educate themselves about love relationships. Never having been encouraged or trained to explore the emotional subtleties of these relationships, they've just too often callously exploited or else unknowingly devalued women.

What is needed (as far as the printed word is concerned) is a rudimentary guidebook for men—a book to help them uncover some of the common emotional minefields they'll be crossing on their different roads to love.

These pages are an attempt at such a guide.

# CHAPTER ONE

# THE EXTINCTION DEMON

A MAN MEETS a woman. They dine together. After an especially good dinner and an especially intense talk, they walk out into the street and anything—the color of someone's scarf, the chrome on a car, a bus pulling away from a curb—takes on a new clarity for them, a *suprarealness*. Love, as songwriters and poets have long known, can literally be an altered state in its earliest stages.

Love's "magic"—its energizing sweetness, its sublime ecstasy—is very real for all who've known it.

One man I interviewed shared with me the "magic" he felt upon meeting a "special" woman:

> I arrived in Paris on a Friday afternoon. I was staying at a hotel right on the Champs-Elysées. I unpacked my baggage, went downstairs, and in front of my hotel there was a sidewalk cafe, so I sat down. I was waiting for a friend who said he'd pick me up at seven o'clock for dinner. So I'm sitting, it's five, five-thirty in Paris, and a woman walks by. I had never picked up a girl on the street. All of the women I met, I'd met socially, through friends. I had never in my life picked a girl up. But this girl walks by, and for the first time in my life I want to talk to her. I want to stop her and talk to her. I can't explain it to you. I'd just arrived in Paris and there she was—walking in a big rush-hour crowd. Then she passed my table and was gone. I sat down and tried to forget about it.

> Later, my friend came and we had dinner together

and then went to a very good musical. We got out of the show at about eleven, and we'd planned on meeting some of his friends at a bar afterward. We walked to the bar. It was a beautiful night, a warm night, and all of a sudden, I don't know what it was, I said to my friend, "Listen, I don't feel well. Do me a favor. You know these people. Go there without me. I'm going home." This was about eleven, eleven-fifteen. So I took a cab. I don't really know why I left. Then I got out of the cab, paid the driver, and I turned around and there she was.

We started talking. She told me her name, a beautiful French name, and she was lovely. I told her about what had happened to me and she said she believed in things like that. It was so fabulous. I could have gone with my friend and never have seen her again. It was too much of a coincidence. She came back to my hotel that night without any ado, without talking about it, and she didn't leave.

Another man, in his eighties when I interviewed him, described his "magical" meeting with a woman. After forty-seven years of marriage, his memories of that first meeting were still vivid:

I was playing my violin at the Roxy on Fifty-third and Broadway in 1927. It was a magnificent music hall. All the big theaters in those days—the Strand, the Rivoli, the Capitol, the Colony, and the Roxy—had a ballet company and an orchestra, a big orchestra that played for the movies because there were no talkies yet. . . . As I was playing my violin—and after playing the same show over and over I could play it from memory—I began to look around a little. But from the orchestra pit, I could only see legs, forty dancing legs on the stage. I couldn't see any of the faces of the ballet dancers. These ballet dancers opened the show. Now women won't like this, but I'm what's known as a leg man. So I'd count all the dancers' legs and I'd look at all of them. But my eyes would always stop when I got to this one particular pair of legs. I kept doing this, looking at all the legs—and they were all very beautiful—but somehow I always ended up stopping at this one pair. So one day, very quietly, I raised myself from my seat so I could see from the pit who this girl was. And there was Becky, this youngster, so young. And, you know, it just kind of touched me. She was completely innocent. She was so beautiful to look at. Truthfully, I knew that day that I wanted to marry her. . . . I'll tell you, and this is true, that over the years, and it's been over forty-five years and that's a very long time . . . well, I won't tell you that I love her more today than when I first met her, but I will tell you that I love her as much now as when I first saw her—legs first, then her face—that day at the Roxy.

Love is a violinist eyeing his beloved ballerina for the first time. Love is a fortuitous meeting on a spring night in Paris. Love is Bogey and Bacall in *To Have and Have Not*. What we're too often never told, though, is that love isn't *always* magical. And especially in the beginning it can be altogether maddening.

Men, in particular, have a difficult time with love during the early phases of a new relationship. This is because love's more expanded states of being are accompanied for them by a terrible though usually unconscious fear.

This is a fear men have of losing their independence in a close relationship. It's the fear, Dr. Rollo May states, "of being totally absorbed by the other, the fear of losing one's self and one's autonomy." I call this fear the Extinction Demon.

One of the early psychoanalysts, Otto Rank, described this fear, this initial demon all men encounter on their different roads to love. He chose to call it the "death fear." Whatever its name, it refers to the fear men have of losing their autonomy in an intimate relationship.

*     *     *

I received a phone call one Saturday night from a friend of a friend. This man, a well-to-do real estate broker in his mid-thirties, knew I was writing a book about "men and love." He apologized for calling me on a weekend, but then said it was urgent; he needed to talk to someone.

He began to tell me how he'd just met a woman and he was sure she was the "one." He'd never been more attracted to anyone in his life. "She has everything," he said. "Looks, poise, sensitivity, empathy, ambition. But you know," he added, "I'm scared to death. I swear, I don't even know who I am anymore. My business—it's the last thing I think about. The relationship's just pulling me all over the place."

He was sharing with me, in the typically inarticulate way these feelings often get expressed, his deepest fears about falling in love. He was telling me that love, at these very early stages, was thrilling. But somehow it was also strangely and uncomfortably unhinging: It was making him feel higher than he'd ever felt but also more disoriented than he generally liked to feel. "I'm losing control" was an expression he used a lot.

If he had had the words available to him, he would have said, "I'm battling the Extinction Demon."

I ended up meeting this man several times after our telephone conversation. And clearly, he'd fallen in love (or at least into a very deep infatuation). Each time we talked, he'd tell me about all the lofty moments he was having with this woman: How they'd just talked for hours, sharing their dreams for their future life together, how they'd told one another they'd never felt more comfortable with anyone else in their lives. But after telling me about all these connected and rapturous moments, he'd invariably start telling me how scared it was all making him.

Prior to meeting her, this man sensed his life needed a change. He was making a lot of money but he still felt unfulfilled. So he'd left his family's business, and with no real plans in mind, he'd traveled around the country, finally settling in a small college town in Southern California. He had friends there; plus, he was thinking of returning to school to study architecture, a longtime passion.

After only two weeks in this idyllic college town, he and Janice had met. And for a while, their relationship felt ecstatic. They spent practically every moment together—making love and talking. It was, Paul later confided, "other-worldly."

There were, of course, little things that bothered them about each other. Janice felt, for instance, that Paul could be a little too rigid—that if he wanted something, he could be inflexible. And there were even times when she felt he could be arrogant. Paul, in turn, felt Janice was sometimes overly critical. But these were small complaints really; nothing their intense love couldn't handle.

Their relationship went along fairly smoothly. But

then, Janice began asking Paul about these mildly irk-some traits. She just wanted to talk about them with him. At that point, Paul very quickly made it clear he wanted no part in her "cross-examinations." His tender feelings immediately vanished the moment she broached either his stubbornness or his condescension. As Paul later said: "I just couldn't handle her prying into my interior life. I knew there was something sincere about what she was doing. But there was also something very critical."

Janice had touched Paul's deepest emotional difficulties and these were issues Paul wasn't ready to explore. He just wasn't ready to be vulnerable with either himself or a woman.

Paul very quickly put up a rigid wall around himself. He became withdrawn—practically inaccessible to Janice. His once overflowing emotions were now coolly reserved. As a result, three months after it had begun, their relationship was over.

These rigid walls, these defenses that Paul (and many other men in similar situations) mobilized are shields from intimacy. They're a man's protection from becoming too close, too self-revealing to a woman. Ultimately, they're what keeps at bay this Extinction Demon. If a man can coolly retreat into his protective shell, the threat of vulnerability, of losing himself in a woman, can be quashed.

\*　　\*　　\*

When I first met my wife-to-be, these initial defenses took the form of an aloof barrier of spirituality. Like many middle-class, college-educated men who came of age in the late sixties, I'd become interested in the philosophies of various Eastern religions. I was a half-sincere spiritual seeker back then; a Hindu one day, a Buddhist the next: A spiritual seeker who knew, because he'd read it somewhere, that "women and gold" were all that kept a man from God. These "spiritual" ideas (on temporary loan to me from such cultural heroes as Alan Watts and Allen Ginsburg) were partly a convenient way for me, I now understand, to prematurely circumvent the complexities and personal risks of human love.

Loving a woman, to my Eastern way of seeing things, was nothing more than another of life's illusions. The desire for sensual pleasures, even for the companionship of women, was, as far as Hindu cosmology and I were concerned, the thorniest obstacle to spiritual liberation. The lure of the flesh became my invulnerable foe; women, dangerous and seductive tigresses at Heaven's gates.

This "spiritual seeker" identity was an admixture of sincere longing, disdain for the materialism of my parents, and an utter fear of my own deepest turmoils and insecurities. But mostly it was a clever way for me to distance myself from women, from the potentially frightening entanglements of intimate relationships.

For other men, I've seen these initial resistances to love take the form of a certain exclusive seriousness they attach to their careers, or else to some gung-ho desire to explore life to its fullest. These men just can't become too involved in a love relationship, they tell themselves, because of either a commitment to a career or to an adventurous lifestyle. But again, whatever form these defenses take, their function is often the same: To ward off a woman's threatening love.

\* \* \*

In the very beginning of a love relationship, when a man is in the company of a new woman he cares about, he'll often try to firm up his sense of himself. He'll do this to allay his unconscious fears of engulfment. He'll subtly (or not so subtly) let the woman know, for example, just how successful he is, or how he wants only a mature and independent relationship from now on in; or, even more classic, he'll offhandedly tell her about all the other women who are anxiously waiting in the wings. Again, men will do this, this re-cementing of their inner defensive walls, because they're simultaneously fearing that this new woman may soon be "too close for comfort."

If these gentler stratagems all fail—and as a relationship intensifies they generally do—men, I've observed, will then resort to more elaborate and often much more cruel defenses. Some men will abruptly pull back their warmth, their previous effusive emotions becoming hardened; or some men will just suddenly start launching into cruel harangues about what they most despise in their new lovers. And some men will simply choose trivial annoyances to prey upon. One man I interviewed told me how he kept complaining to his girlfriend about her *klutziness* around tools. Another man confided how all of a sudden he just couldn't cope with his girlfriend's slightly pointed and asymmetrical chin. And both these men, in vacillating moments of earnestness and confusion, told me these were valid reasons to withdraw their love from these once "special" women.

What was happening to both of these men was that as they were intensifying their emotional involvements with these women, neither one was quite ready for the experience. They were experiencing love's earliest advances not as some divine grace, but rather—and this is the Extinction Demon-at-work—as an ever-encroaching threat to their inner equilibrium.

Another man, recently divorced but legally separated for many years, was living with a new woman when I interviewed him. He cared for her, but there was no way in hell, he told me, he'd ever marry her. "I'll only marry a woman if she's into a career, if her head's together, and if she isn't going to be bugging me about anything." His list of prerequisites went on to include beauty, wealth, and no commitment to monogamy. It was clear he was emotionally distancing himself from the woman he was living with by setting such standards for a future spouse.

This very common male distancing stratagem I call the "Bionic Woman Syndrome." By creating an idealized perfect specimen—one that exists only in his imagination—a man can put off, just a little longer, the joys and pains of being vulnerable to the flesh-and-blood women he's either living with or dating. This Bionic Woman Syndrome is, simply, another of the walls men put up to keep women out.

A friend of mine, struggling to make a commitment to a woman he's been dating, admitted experiencing this Bionic Woman Syndrome. "It's like I'm looking for a perfect fit in an off-the-rack world," he smiled. "And I know I'm doing it just so I can stall a little longer."

With my wife, I had my own well-stocked arsenal of ploys to protect myself when we first met, cruel stratagems to stop myself from loving her. Like most men, I feared—and this is the Extinction Demon—that if Vivien could work her way into my insides, then I'd be finished. All the illusions about how "together" I was, about how "spiritually" evolved I was, would be exploded. And then I'd just have to be myself and that was too frightening.

So to preserve those cherished self-delusions, I had to ferociously yet subtly resist her. And to do that, I'd find her clothes, for instance, unappealing and that would allow me to sufficiently turn off to her (and then I wouldn't have to love her anymore). Or something about her appearance—her slightly enlarged ears or maybe the purplish rings under her eyes when she hadn't slept enough—would quickly shut down my love. It was a strange and eccentric assortment of picayune traits I'd then sadistically bloat into major character blights to stop myself from loving her. . . . It was, again, one of my unconscious ways of keeping love at a safe distance.

\*    \*    \*

There are two other classic defenses men employ to keep love at arm's length. Frequently, a man will complain to a woman during the early phases of a relationship that he can't be monogamous. It feels, he says, too constricting for him. In some cases, this is a very real and tormenting struggle. But in many cases, it's just another way for a man to keep the Extinction Demon at bay—a way for a man to further resist a woman's love. (This defense will be explored in greater depth in Chapter Six.)

The other very common defense is something I call the "Loss of Love Excuse." A lot of men, especially at the beginning of a relationship, are genuinely perplexed when they feel themselves losing love for a woman. They wake up one morning, and for a variety of reasons (often having nothing to do with the specific woman they're with) they just don't feel the same magic anymore. Many men then take this temporary loss of love to be a sign—a sign that it's time to end their relationship.

But the Extinction Demon's convenient and skewed logic is prompting this faulty conclusion. What these men don't know (and what the Extinction Demon doesn't want them to know) is that this sort of vicissitudes, these risings and fallings in the amount of love a man feels for his partner, is a normal part of any romantic relationship. Indeed, in the course of a long-term relationship, a man (or a woman) will fall in and out of love with their mate many, many times. But again, afraid of becoming too dependent on a woman, many men end their relationships at the very first signs that love is on the wane.

The following interview with a thirty-year-old man—a social worker from Boston—graphically illustrates this often subtle dynamic:

> I met Joanne about seven months ago. She's a high-powered lawyer. A mutual friend introduced us.
>
> Joanne wasn't the type of woman I'm usually attracted to. She's more normal, if you know what I mean. My past has been filled with some fairly strange ladies, really needy types who didn't have it together in the world. I would play, you know, "big daddy" to them. But then I met Joanne, who's really successful and independent.
>
> I got into this thing with Joanne. We'd spend most of our weekends together. We'd stay at one of our apartments. And, I swear, it would get weird. I'd look at Joanne and I'd really love her; I'd feel really great. But then, in just a little while, I'd look at her again

and I'd, well, I'd lose the good feelings. I'd just be looking at her and thinking to myself that she wasn't really right for me; that she wasn't hip enough or mysterious enough. It felt *schitzy*.

I'd get into these really wavering kinds of thoughts. And I guess I felt that if I loved Joanne, really loved her, then I wouldn't be feeling all these swings. You know, I'd just love her and that would be that.

I finally talked to her about it. It was haunting me. You know, I'd find myself loving our coziness—watching old movies, making breakfast. But then, there'd be these thoughts; that we weren't right for each other; I didn't really love her; she was too straight for me. I even felt I should leave her because I'd just end up hurting her anyway.

Well, these were like little dark pockets in my head. When I finally told her about them, and it took me a few months, it felt like a heavy weight was coming off my head. By her reaction, I could tell she didn't feel they were much to worry about, just part of the ups and downs of any relationship. She went through something like it, she said; just not as intense.

It's not like these thoughts are now gone forever. They just don't feel so threatening. I don't have to act on them.

It's always hard, of course, especially at the very beginning of a new relationship, to know if the doubts and reservations you're feeling about someone are genuine or not. Are they real or are they just the Extinction Demon at work? Are they things you'll genuinely have a hard time with later on or are they just superficial obstacles you're putting in love's way, the result of being afraid of getting too close to someone?

All you can really do at this point in a relationship is

to patiently sift through these doubts; and then, as honestly as possible, decide which are the twenty-four-carat doubts and which are the fool's gold. But by knowing some of the more common forms of fool's gold—some of the more common defenses the Extinction Demon mobilizes—it will at least be easier to discern between deeper-level doubts and the more superficial ones.

This Extinction Demon, the fear of losing autonomy in a love relationship, is experienced differently by every man. For some, it's experienced as if the glue that's previously held them together was beginning to lose hold a bit. They feel a little more vaporous, less solid somehow. For others, it can be an even more threatening feeling, as if they're drowning—the feeling that they're too quickly being swept away from the shores of themselves.

Just how threateningly a man experiences this demon depends on many factors. But how comfortable (or how uncomfortable) he is with intimacy is clearly pivotal.

Fundamentally, the Extinction Demon is a primal fear of intimacy. It's the fear that if a man is too intimate, then he'll somehow end up losing himself (and his control) in a romantic relationship. So if a man has never known real intimacy—the spontaneous sharing of his deeper self—say with his mother or his father, or later with a brother or a sister, or even later with a friend, then he'll invariably have a wretched time battling this demon: Never having experienced intimacy as a nonthreatening and salutory experience in any of his earlier relationships, it will be painful for him to experience it later on with a woman.

Dr. Otto Kernberg, a well-known psychiatrist, along with a number of other researchers, has carefully observed how this ability to experience intimacy in our adult relationships is complicated by our earliest familial interactions. According to these theorists, just as, say, the developing body of a fetus or an infant needs to be fed regularly and nutritiously by its mother, the nascent self and personality of an infant also needs to be appropriately cared for: Our *selves*—our senses of who we are—need a stable diet of protective and engaging parental attention in order to develop into healthy adults; i.e., adults capable of experiencing intimate relationships. And, conversely, if this self—this at first chaotic and undifferentiated brawl of emotions, ideas, and passions—is ignored or given only superficial or sporadic parental attention, then it will grow strangely or stuntedly, or sometimes even not at all; its ability to create meaningful adult relationships is thereby severely impaired.

Dr. Kernberg has gone so far as to posit a sort of mental health continuum based on this premise. Schizophrenics, he states, who probably received very little healthy parental attention, often have a total incapacity to create genital and tender relations with other human beings. And at the extreme other end of the spectrum are people who were given reliable and sensitive parental attention. These are people, according to Dr. Kernberg, who can integrate sexuality and tenderness into a stable adult relationship.

Somewhere between these two extremes, of course, lie all the rest of us.

So it's especially our parents, by either engaging and respecting or else by ignoring and punishing our deeper selves, who ultimately prepare us (or who fail to prepare us) for our adult romantic relationships. They're the ones who offer us our earliest training—by the way they relate to us and by the way they relate to each other—in how to be emotionally engaged (or disengaged), in how to be honest (or dishonest), and in how to be affectionate (or cold) in a love relationship. Because of our parents, we bring to our adult romantic relationships basically sound or basically faulty selves. And because of them, our wrestlings with this Extinction Demon are either tolerable or excruciating.

\* \* \*

After a man meets a woman, he'll inevitably be in for a battle with this Extinction Demon. And his early battles are often the fiercest. But these first bouts usually subside as he gets used to surrendering some of his autonomy for the greater pay-offs of a relationship. This Extinction Demon relaxes its tentacles, in other words, as Nena O'Neal, co-author of *Open Marriage,* states, "when a man learns that his freedom to grow does not come from refusing to enter into committed relationships but instead in the capacity to become himself within the relationship."

This Extinction Demon starts spewing fire again, however, immediately after the question of marriage arises. It's a simple formula: As a man's fears of being engulfed in a long-term marriage are activated, his resistances to that relationship increase.

One man I interviewed told me how he periodically announced his marriage plans, only to call his friends two weeks later to postpone them. He just didn't feel emotionally ready for a long-term relationship. This sort of seesawing is very common for men on the verge of marriage. They're enacting what I call the Extinction Demon Spasms—three steps forward in the direction of marriage, followed by two steps backward.

Other men—men who've been living with the same woman for many years but who don't like to even mention the idea of getting married—are caught in still another of the Extinction Demon's dances. These men often love the women they're with. But their love still isn't strong enough, or maybe they feel their partner's love isn't trustworthy enough, for them to give up more of their independence.

These men, incidentally, will sometimes defend the fact that they're "still living with" and "not yet married to" these women by pointing out the meaninglessness of a marriage certificate: *Who needs a piece of paper to corroborate love?* Their argument's sound. But what's often behind their argument is their inability to make that deeper plunge into a more committed relationship. The step from "living together" to "getting married," simply, is a larger step than the Extinction Demon is allowing them to make.

\* \* \*

Like many men, when I first met my wife-to-be, I battled the Extinction Demon. Like many men, too, I was also—I just didn't know it—falling in love.

I should have known. I had, I now see, an obvious symptom: A lightness of spirit—singing along, at the top of my lungs, to the "Top 40" AM hits. And there were other telltale signs: I started compulsively brushing my teeth and eating less garlic; I started wearing tighter-fitting clothes; I kept my bedroom clean. I saved magazine articles pertaining to film (Vivien's greatest passion). I even bought Vivien a car one day, surprising her with a check for a hundred and fifty dollars, the amount she owed a friend who'd sold her his junker.

People used to tell me (and still do) that "falling in love" is a Hollywood fabrication, that it has no basis in everyday reality. It's merely a "fantasy trip," something that only happens, at least in that "magical" way, to film stars. Even several of my women friends, disillusioned with love, halfheartedly began telling me that the experience of "falling in love" is apocryphal.

But despite what these cynical or disillusioned people told me, I knew—soon after I met Vivien—that I was falling in love with her.

FALLING IN LOVE. It's a misnomer really because at the beginning anyway, you don't *fall.* It's more like you jerkily shuttle between poles—an open, expanded "everything-will-work-out-because-this-feels-right" pole and a closed, contracted "this-is-crazy-and-if-I-don't-stop-this-now-I'm-going-to-really-mess-myself-up" pole.

\* \* \*

The first time I ever met Vivien was eight years ago, a sunny October day. I was on my way to a lecture about Nepal. A friend who'd trekked in the Himalayas was presenting a slide show. As I walked across the New England town common that afternoon, munching on a sugarless health food candy bar and probably inwardly counting the inhalations and exhalations of my breath (one of the many Buddhist meditations I flirted with back then), another part of me was feeling very wobbly: That was the part of me that, unbeknownst to me, was in search of a wife.

"Do you know where Merrill Hall is?" she asked me. She was wearing a green ski sweater and, like a high school kid in the fifties, she was carrying some books in the crook of her arm. Her brown eyes, hiding behind way-too-large wire-rimmed glasses, were trying to make things easy for me. They were open, welcoming, almost too eagerly so.

She was on her way to see *Some Like It Hot* starring Marilyn Monroe, Jack Lemmon, and Tony Curtis. I was on my way to hear a lecture about the snow-capped peaks of Nepal. And truly, that says it all about who we both were when we first met that October afternoon.

I was, at least in my fantasies, a dispassionate Buddhist (again, a Hindu one day, a Buddhist the next) yearning to escape to some snow-capped mountain hermitage in Tibet. She—well, she'd once seen a mountain hermitage in Frank Capra's film *Lost Horizon*, but that's where her interest in things of the spirit stopped.

At least that's what my spiritual pride was telling me back then. Looking back on that first day, though, it's clear I was the one who was really afraid of what the spiritual life was all about. Love.

I was afraid of feeling my feelings back then. I was afraid of being honest. I was, in other words (and it's something my subsequent research has shown me), like many of the men in America.

I was, simply, an emotional primitive when Vivien and I met eight years ago. I could detect only two broad and vague categories of feelings: *Good* feelings or *bad* feelings.

Vivien was twenty-three back then, a recent graduate of Pomona College. She'd been living in this New England college town for only a couple of weeks and doing odd jobs—waitressing and modeling for art classes—

and occasionally, like the day we met, sitting in on some film courses.

It was how a lot of people spent their first year or two out of college back in the early seventies; just scraping a living on the safe fringes of a university town. It was, in fact, exactly what I'd been doing. But I'd already been doing it, some would have said (my parents), longer than you're supposed to.

Anyway, there I was, standing next to Vivien that first day we met, silently putting down *Some Like It Hot* (thinking to myself it was a "lesser" pleasure than a lecture on Nepal). But somewhere else—somewhere way back there—behind all my icy Buddhist thinking, I could feel a very frightened man who very much needed the playful warmth of this vulnerable woman.

I ended up walking Vivien to the auditorium where *Some Like It Hot* was being shown. I walked her there, I now know, partly because I felt she was attracted to me; partly because I was struggling (as contradictory as it may sound) to be a more spontaneously giving person back then; and partly—though I wasn't at all aware of this at the time—because I was very lonely.

Delivering her to Merrill Hall, my final and somewhat formal words to her were, "So I guess it's come to a parting of the ways." But she'd have none of that. Her rejoinder, "Why?"

In that one word, she was unabashedly telling me she was interested in me and wanted to see me again.

A few months later, when she confided she'd known exactly where *Some Like It Hot* was being shown that day, I was floored. She'd spotted me from a distance, had instinctively felt she wanted to talk to me, and then had pretended to need directions. . . . An almost too-Hollywood ruse but it worked.

Henry Miller once wrote, "Men always say, 'The women I select.' I say they select *us*. I give myself no credit for selecting. Sure, I ran after them, I struggled, and all that, but I can't say, 'Oh, that's gotta be mine. Now that's the type I want and I'm gonna get it.' No, it doesn't work that way."

\*     \*     \*

When my lecture and Vivien's movie were over that day, I went back to Merrill Hall to meet her. Standing outside the auditorium, I spotted her just as she came out, and I watched her take off her glasses and let down her hair. She swears she saw me, too, slip off my wire-rimmed glasses and tuck them into my shirt pocket.

Our first struggles at conversation were awkward and choppy. I was, I remember, being interviewed: Vivien, the talk show host; me, the feigning-to-be-humble celeb.

VIVIEN: What do you do?
STEVE: I'm a writer.
VIVIEN (very enthusiastically): A writer?
STEVE (struggling to be low-key): Yeah.
VIVIEN (even more enthusiastically): Who do you write for?
STEVE (still low-key): A couple of places.
AWKWARD PAUSE . . . Vivien now looking at Steve questioningly . . . FINALLY—
STEVE: You know, *The Boston Globe, New Times.*
VIVIEN (effusively, as if the ghost of Henry James had suddenly arisen): R-E-A-L-L-Y?
STEVE (still aloof but loving the flattery): Just a bunch of magazines.

After an hour's worth of questions and answers, we headed back to our cars. I felt very awkward at that point. If I accidentally brushed up against her, it felt like one of those games sixth grade science fair contestants rig up with a nail and two wires: If you touch one of the two wires while trying to move the nail through the maze, ZAP—you either get an electric shock or a house bell goes off.

I was twenty-six then. It was time, I sensed, to know what love was really all about. I needed to know why Bogey, for instance, was so forlorn when Ingrid Bergman didn't show up at that Paris train station in *Casablanca*. What heights had he known with her that could cause such suffering?

For years, I'd listened to dozens of old rock 'n' roll songs, to dozens of Sinatra ballads—songs about the loss of love, songs about people finding love. But I'd never found love. At least, not the sort of transporting love those songwriters and screenwriters were talking about. I'd known a certain type of love with my first wife: *companionship*. (I'd married that first time when I was just twenty years old.) We were "buddies," not "lovers," though. Much of our young lives together had been spent exploring the world: We'd bought an old tobacco farm in the Tennessee mountains. Later, we'd traveled throughout India; finally, we'd settled in Massachusetts—me to become a writer, she, a potter.

But that brotherly-sisterly sort of love, precious as it was to me at that time in my life, was a far cry, I always painfully sensed, from seeing myself in a gin joint in Casablanca years after we'd separated, pining away for her. . . . What was this other love, this realer love; this love that wasn't just safe and chummy but that was electric?

After we met, Vivien and I spent a lot of time together. And a lot happens when you spend extended time with someone you love or with someone you're learning to love (or even with someone whose love you're resisting). After a while, all the familiar ways of relating—chitchatting about the weather, comparing political opinions and movie tastes, trading scoops of gossip, even sharing your heartfelt autobiographies—begin to exhaust themselves. Under normal circumstances, that's usually when two people start feeling more than a little anxious with each other. That's even, possibly, when they stop seeing each other. But during the falling in love phase of our relationship, we worked out an agreement: To give each other the freedom to share whatever feelings, urges, or thoughts we were experiencing. By doing that, we were acting, I think, on a universal desire: The strong urge to share our most vulnerable selves. (Typically, it's women, I've observed, who are the first to really expose their most private fears and desires during this falling in love phase of a relationship. Women, too, are usually the first to express their unconditional affection—making them the first to be truly vulnerable in a relationship. The entire development of intimacy in a love relationship, therefore, is generally pioneered by women. A man, meanwhile, will usually listen to and reassure a woman during this phase of a relationship, as she confides her insecurities to him; the thrill of sexuality making him a better listener than he's ever been in his life. But again, it's the woman who's really doing all the dirty work, who's vulnerably exposing all her dirty laundry, as it were.)

So we had an agreement: To not close down shop, to not flee from intimacy, even when all the conventions of normal relating were sometimes telling us to. And because of that agreement, it would occasionally feel as if Vivien and I were stepping into new terrains: Those early months together, in other words, when the Extinction Demon would relax its tentacles, could sometimes feel ecstatic. Love's openness, love's warmth—its relaxed and charged glow—would grant us a visit. At those moments, each of us would know we'd finally met our true mate.

But unfortunately, love didn't allow us to just sit back and lap up its bounty. No. The falling in love phase of any romantic relationship, I learned, is complicated by a very strong desire to get lost in all that love. . . . Which brings us to the Fusion Demon, that deep urge in men to lose themselves in their wives or girlfriends.

# CHAPTER TWO

# THE FUSION DEMON

PSYCHOLOGISTS AND POETS have long known that there exists in men an almost primitive urge to be merged with their lovers, some strong and usually unconscious desire to lose themselves in their mates. At some very deep level, men sense in themselves, as the psychologist Dorothy Dinnerstein explains, "A temptation to give way to a ferocious and voracious dependence on women." This sometimes overpowering male urge I call the Fusion Demon. (This word, *fusion,* is currently used in physics. It describes any process whereby diverse elements are merged. It's a term, too, that family therapists have recently adopted.)

Most men, at a relationship's outset, vehemently resist love. But then, at some point, when they finally stop resisting, they end up falling desperately in love: Once a woman gets through a man's defensive walls, men are likely to fall hopelessly in love.

This tendency, this strong tendency in men to become increasingly dependent on their women, is usually masked at first. Men will try to deny their dependency needs at the beginning of a relationship, and they'll do this by treating their wives or girlfriends as if *they* were the excessively fragile and dependent ones. But as much as a man tries to play the part of the strong lover, at some deeper place he's often feeling very vulnerable and very dependent.

Now a certain amount—indeed, a large amount—of mutual dependency is necessary for creating intimacy in love relationships. We need to be able to express our neediness to each other, our primal dependency on each other, and not be condemned or banished for doing so.

But the question is: How not to be too dependent but dependent enough? And, unfortunately, too many men err in the direction of becoming overly dependent.

What is this Fusion Demon, this overdependence about? Why are men so drawn to being *fused* with their spouses? "The force behind fusion," Dr. Thomas F. Fogarty, a family therapist, explains, "is the desperate hope of filling one's emptiness by uniting with or taking something from another person." It's a sense of inner emptiness, therefore, a feeling that the pylons supporting their ego are either insubstantial or else totally nonexistent, that propels many men into becoming overly dependent on women.

One man I interviewed, a thirty-four-year-old Los Angeles lawyer, spoke to me about these hollow, inner feelings:

> On the weekends, I'm often the last person to leave the beach. That's when I feel it. I'm walking back to my car and I feel—well, I feel like I don't exist. I dunno, like I'm some sort of Martian who doesn't know what the hell he's doing down here. . . . I can usually make the feelings go away by getting in my car and throwing on a tape. But I know it's there . . . I just try not to feel it.
>
> A couple of years ago, when those feelings hit, I'd go out and pick up a woman. I got into, you know, a sex binge; a different woman every other night. No way was I going to stay alone in my apartment.

This man sensed his inner emptiness. He knew, deep down, things just weren't right.

This sense of inner emptiness, these feelings that blindly propel many men into either superficial sexual binges or else into overly dependent relationships, have, unfortunately, become more and more widespread in our culture. As Christopher Lasch, the author of *The Culture of Narcissism*, states, "The sense of inner emptiness combined with a dependence on the vicarious warmth provided by others, along with a fear of that dependence, is common." It's the psychological baggage too many of us today—men and women alike—are carrying.

Making matters worse is the fact that most men are barely aware of these feelings in themselves. Their lives, in fact, are often spent frantically avoiding them.

\*   \*   \*

In my own case, right before I met my wife-to-be, my life was relatively calm. Writing for magazines—the constant hustle of being a freelance writer, the satisfaction of seeing my name in print—was something I enjoyed. But when I met Vivien, and the intensity of our chemistry became so overwhelmingly apparent to me, everything else started to pale, until eventually nothing had any meaning to me anymore: Seeing old friends, writing articles—they all lost their charge. For the first time in my life, really, I was experiencing love's acceptance, love's openness. At last, I was floating in the stuff of romantic movies and Sinatra ballads, and I wanted—who wouldn't?—as much of it as I could get.

So this "paling effect" of young love felt wonderful for a while. It was as if I'd been temporarily released from all the repetitive and humdrum acts of day-to-day living. But, then, much too quickly, because of the Fusion Demon—this powerful urge to lose myself in Vivien—the ecstasy started to vanish. And that was when my newfound love started to overwhelm me—when I started experiencing love not as any kind of sharing but rather as a wretched craving that could never be satisfied.

How had I gotten to such a miserably dependent state? I'd begun our love affair, I'd thought, so cautiously, my spiritual pretensions doing a fairly good job of protecting me from falling in love. And when they'd failed, I'd begun to bloat Vivien's smallest foibles into major stumbling blocks and that worked for a while. But when that ploy also failed, there was just no turning back anymore. So I'd opened to all the love. I'd loved the love.

Getting lost in all the love was just something I never expected.

*     *     *

One woman, a twenty-two-year-old college senior, told me about her involvement with a man who had succumbed to the Fusion Demon:

> We started dating and for a while it really clicked. I respected Peter. He was a warm guy, really honest, not like a lot of the guys you meet. But what happened was he started falling in love faster than me.
>
> A few months into the relationship, I started getting sort of scared. I'd just never seen anything like it. This guy who I really thought had it together, all of a sudden was acting like a baby. He wanted me to marry him. But when I said "no," he wouldn't stop

crying. So I held him. You know, and for a few days
this went on. But then, it all started switching to anger
and then he just started going nuts on me, slamming
doors, cursing, throwing things.

He'd flip and then he'd just come back into my
room and tell me he had to sleep next to me, that he
couldn't be alone: He'd be this puppy dog one minute, this helpless, vulnerable thing, but then he'd just
become an angry monster.

This sort of wild mood vacillations—anger at your
mate one moment, followed by unmanageable vulnerability—often means a man is in the jaws of the Fusion
Demon.

This Fusion Demon—the psychological hunger that
makes a man start wanting love *too* much—is a demon
that subverts a balanced, human love because anything
you become addicted to, you end up not just loving.
After a while you begin to hate whatever it is you need
so much.

\*   \*   \*

Once a man has established his primary relationship
with a woman, he'll often start to abandon all his other
relationships. This further exacerbates male dependency on women. In this process, a man often ends up
becoming a social isolate, his wife his only life connection.

Countless men I spoke with told me how they had
only superficial relationships with everyone except their
wives. Wives, on the other hand, usually had close
friends, other women they could confide in.

One irate wife complained to me about her excessively dependent husband:

He's such a needy person, so dependent. He just depends on me for every goddamn thing. It drives me up the wall, absolutely drives me up the wall. He doesn't have any interests of his own, any friendships of his own. He sits and sleeps in that chair or in that TV room whenever we don't have a plan for a particular night. He's always asking me what do I have planned, what are we doing tonight. . . . You know, I do the social planning but it would be nice if he took an interest sometimes. I just can't hack being sucked at all the time.

This exclusive dependency that many men develop for their wives is, again, what can become dangerous in a marriage. It's what causes a man's love to become clutchier and more possessive. Ultimately, it's what ruins many marriages. This sort of clutchiness, as the novelist May Sarton says, "is the surest way to murder love."

\*     \*     \*

It's rough going for a man when he's in the throes of this demon. Again, the mood swings he's experiencing—anger one moment, unmanageable vulnerability the next—can be tormenting. To free himself from these potent claws of the Fusion Demon, he has to first come to terms with his own expanses of inner emptiness; those hollow feelings his desperate and clinging love wants to cover up. He needs to take, in other words, a long and serious look at himself, at his inner depths.

This part of a man's "love journey," this process of self-examination, is, essentially, a solo expedition. It's work a man needs to do alone. And no matter how much the woman he's involved with is willing to encourage him in this undertaking, there's really no way around the solitary nature of this task. "No matter how much we care for another," state George and Nena O'Neill, "we cannot do their inner growing for them. In caring, we become enabling factors in one another's growth, but most of the actual work of growth we must undertake on our own. Each person must work through his own style of self-development."

How to begin this process? How can a man start on his journey of self-examination? If a man feels, even for a brief moment, some small flutter of inner shakiness—some uncertainty, say, when his wife or girlfriend recounts to him a triumph of hers at work or just reports that her life feels full—then very possibly this can be his first step, his entranceway into the more vulnerable parts of himself. Men need to look at these kinds of moments in their relationships, these moments when they feel either vaguely or acutely threatened.

If a man can then earnestly look at these fragile parts of himself without rationalizing them away, or ignoring them, or else inflicting them on his wife, he'll have started on his journey of self-development and self-exploration.

These long denied parts of himself (e.g., his fear of dependency, his feelings of jealousy, his inability to express tenderness) will, of course, all feel unwieldy, even monstrous at first. It's always frightening when a man first glimpses these weaknesses in himself. But as he slowly gets used to examining them and not running away from them, they'll begin to lose their bite.

This process of self-examination adds solid muscle to a man's inner core: By reclaiming the lost and vulnerable parts of himself, he starts filling in his inner emptiness. And ultimately, it's this strong inner core that allows each one of us some healthy degree of inner detachment, some center of ourselves that's inviolate—some part of ourselves that can stand on its own in intimate relationships without the need to be fused with others.

In the past ten years or so, it has become a little too easy to be flippant about this whole process of self-examination. A lavish smorgasbord of therapeutic slogans have flooded into our everyday speech during these years; and what's happened is these slogans have replaced the hard work, the genuine struggle of inner exploration. Instead of sincerely trying to wrestle with these painful demons, many men now just spew mass-produced slogans: *I need my space . . . It's just not happening between us . . . Things got too heavy.*

A lot of the men I interviewed for this book felt content to stop their inner explorations with these sorts of statements. Countless psychotherapists, too, mentioned this fact: That their male clients often conveniently danced along the surface of their deepest torments by employing these shibboleths and slogans of the "Human Potential Movement."

\*     \*     \*

The Extinction Demon and the Fusion Demon are demons men are constantly battling all along their journeys to love. And often, these demons collide: This need and desire to be deeply connected to one woman (the Fusion Demon) versus the desire to keep their "freedom" and not be tied down (the Extinction Demon).

These fears are major psychological themes for any man. They're fears, too, that aren't present only at the beginning of a love relationship. They exist, unfortunately, all throughout a romantic relationship, making their most painful appearances at certain nodal points: When it's time to decide whether or not to get married . . . when it's time to decide whether or not to have a child . . . when it's time to decide whether or not to have an affair.

In a deeper sense, men never really finish their battles with the Extinction Demon or the Fusion Demon. The fear of entrapment and the pull toward dependency accompany them throughout their lives. But, over the years, as a man surrenders more and more to the love he feels for his spouse, and as he slowly acquires more and more self-knowledge, the intensity of his battles will die down.

We all walk a tightrope in love. The Extinction Demon is pushing us one way, far away from love, while the Fusion Demon is pushing us the other way, toward too much dependency. And the question always is: How to stay balanced, how to stay on the wire?

Clearly, we can accomplish this balancing act only by knowing who we are: And to do that, we first have to locate what's genuinely ours, and then we have to differentiate what's ours from our spouse's. It's a very delicate process: If you differentiate yourself too much from your spouse, you lose your relationship. But if you don't differentiate yourself enough, you lose yourself.

# CHAPTER THREE

# THE
# ANGER
# DEMON

W HAT FOLLOWS IS an interview with a forty-year-
old theatrical agent from Los Angeles. It
serves as a vivid introduction to the Anger Demon:

Right now both my wife and I have reached a sort
of plateau and we've seen that we've established patterns. You know, at some time in your life everything
is in flux and all your dreams are in the future. But at
a certain age you begin to realize that patterns are
being formed and that where I'm at now is roughly
where I'm going to be in say fifteen years. And at that
point people begin pouting. That's where my wife
and I are now. So there are great tensions in our
marriage now because we're both reexamining what
we want. You start asking yourselves how far is all this
from where your fantasies were when it first started.

From my point of view, our life isn't too far from
where I wanted it to be. But for Barbara it's very far.

Barbara's a very successful TV writer in Los
Angeles, an Emmy winner, so she has a very good
income. But, you know, we have two kids in private
school and all the accoutrements that go along with
that. Plus, we spend an enormous amount of money
on household help. So right there—the kids' school
bill comes to $8,000 a year and the help is like $7,000
a year—is $15,000 from our net which eats up over
twenty grand of our gross. So essentially, Barbara
wants me to earn more money. That's really the crux
of most of our disputes.

Now by my standards, I think I'm a great success—but that's cutting the cloth to fit the body. I enjoy my work. I really enjoy the independence I have. I could certainly make more money from my business but that would make me responsible to too many people which would ruin my independence. God knows, I'd love to be a millionaire. I have nothing at all against money. But if you have to lose too much to get what you want, forget it.

This money thing makes us very nasty to each other. There's lots of resentment. She resents that I don't want to work harder to make more money. I resent her for wanting me to change my lifestyle so she can have what she wants. And all this resentment leads to punishing-type actions. You know, screw him if he doesn't want to cooperate and so on and so on.

I really think all this bickering about finances could eventually do in the marriage. You know, I really don't object to her desires. I just object to being punished for not satisfying them. And the problem isn't really money so much as it is personalities. On a subliminal level, you're always fighting to be the power source in your relationship. And if money was plentiful then we'd both find something else to hassle about.

\*       \*       \*

Like many couples, this man and his wife had already wrangled too many times with this turbulent demon. Another couple, Allen and Beverly, spoke to me about their first encounters with this demon. At the time of our interview, they'd been married only ten months:

ALLEN: I had a sense that I was going to marry

her pretty early on. It felt pretty solid. We had both had a number of relationships before we met and we both pretty much knew that the next time was going to be *the* time. You know, we weren't playing around and we had both reached the point where we had some sense of our own vulnerabilities, fuck-ups, dynamics. It was all very *adult* in the beginning, very mature. But then some of the junk started coming out.

About five months after we met, we were going to Canada, and as we're packing, Beverly all of a sudden started getting crazy about something. I had never lived with someone who started screaming. Screaming, screaming, screaming. It was about whether or not to buy a chicken and she's running her mouth off like a maniac. So I pulled her out of the car and I never found myself wanting so much to absolutely slam the living shit out of a woman. So I'm yelling, not realizing all the time I'm becoming a bigger nut. I had gotten angry before and I had screamed and I had gotten hysterical but I never had anyone become a nut and turn me into one. And that's what began to creep into our relationship. We had already worked through a lot of stuff in order to be honest together but there was a lot more stuff to get into.

BEVERLY: My getting crazy with the chicken wasn't just my getting crazy with the chicken. It was me reacting to something in Allen and him reacting back. Allen goes through periods that are kind of immersions in work but in a way they don't feel just like an immersion in work. They feel like a real pushing away of me. And it always happens right before we're about to take a big vacation. There'll be two weeks when we're supposed to be getting maps, packing, but somehow it just so happens Allen has a mammoth project to finish. And he's literally up twenty-four hours a day for two weeks.

One of the things we've discovered about some of the anger that goes back and forth between us—and often it's really crazy and rageful like the chicken incident—is that it's our way of getting away from ourselves. The rage that's generated is from things I don't want to deal with about myself or what Allen doesn't want to deal with about himself. Getting angry is just a way of getting away from our own skins.

My reseach has shown me that most couples tend to fight about very similar issues—money, sex, social plans, in-laws, housework. These are the sorts of issues that ignite fights. I watched one husband, for example, yell at his wife for being too generous. She'd bought, he felt, a too-lavish gift for a friend's birthday. I watched another husband become enraged because his wife arranged a social engagement with people he didn't like. And I watched one young husband practically go berserk when his wife mentioned she wanted her widowed mother to visit for the weekend.

These are volatile issues for any relationship. But what's important to know is that these seemingly external issues, if traced back far enough, can be seen to have highly explosive fuses—fuses originating in each of our deepest and most vulnerable parts: The Anger Demon is exacerbated by external issues. Its most flammable fuel, though, is more subterranean.

A fight about money, for instance, I saw in myself and in other men, usually wasn't just a fight about money. No. Fighting about money often quickly ignites much deeper issues; namely, a man's deepest feelings of being inadequate in the world. This sense of inadequacy, this feeling of being unsuccessful or unambitious, is what then excessively fuels many marital battles: Not wanting to look at his feelings of inadequacy, a man will simply choose to rant and rave about his wife's spendthrift habits.

Sometimes, too, a fight about money will be nothing but a way for a man to keep the Extinction Demon at bay. Many couples, when they first begin to talk about pooling their financial resources, often end up arguing about money. But what's really causing these money fights is each partner's inner battle with autonomy and dependency. Money, in these cases, just becomes symbolic of these deeper issues—of resisting or surrendering to an intimate relationship.

Fights about sex are similarly deceptive. Couples who fight about sex aren't usually fighting just about sex. One man I interviewed, a thirty-year-old commercial photographer, explained it this way:

> Our biggest conflict is a sexual conflict. The problem really is that we have no sexual relationship at the moment. I know that Janet just doesn't feel like having sex right now and so I don't even bother making advances anymore.
>
> We used to look at it as just a sexual problem and so I attributed all my anger at her as being caused by this bottled-up sexuality. But now I know it's deeper than that. I'll tell you: I can live with having no sex, at least for a while longer. But what I can't live with is the feeling that Janet's rejecting me because she thinks I'm a *creep*.

This man's constant rage at his girlfriend was obviously being triggered by something much more potent than being sexually rejected by her. His rage clearly had its most explosive roots in his deeper-level feelings that he was worthless and inept.

Sexual rejection is always painful. But when it's excruciatingly connected to our most vulnerable parts, when it so easily can tip the scales of our self-esteem, then it's hell and the pain is often unbearable. And many men, in order to avoid that pain, simply cover it all over with a blind and boundless rage: That anger allows men some brief moments of power or temporary relief, when what they're really experiencing is utter vulnerability.

Anger and vulnerability are bedmates. In his very first battles with the Extinction Demon and the Fusion Demon, a man will use anger as a powerful smoke-screen, as a way to avoid experiencing either his own growing vulnerability to a woman or else his own inadequacies. But even later on, after a couple's first rounds with the Extinction Demon have subsided, this deep link between anger and vulnerability persists. As a thirty-two-year-old clinical psychologist—speaking about his own marital relationship—observed:

> We've already had three divorces. One lasted three-and-a-half days. It was horrible. You know, when you can't get off the phone but when you're yelling at each other. You're seething but you can't get off the damn phone: When it's "I can't hang up on her—she'll call me back anyway—so if I try to hang up on her and the fight's not settled, well, I'm not going to be able to do my work anyway." It's

terrible—terrible because there's just something in those moments when you realize you're not autonomous in this world. There's somebody linked into your guts at a very primitive level and if you don't get it OK with them, then nothing else is going to work. You realize you're totally helpless.

I spent an evening with a couple recently, and right from the start there was a palpable tension between them. Apparently, they'd been fighting all day. During dinner, whenever something had to be negotiated between them, it immediately became a fight: Putting their four-year-old daughter to sleep degenerated into a heated debate between two conflicting schools of child-rearing. The main course, too, was no longer a meal but rather a competitive culinary battleground. Their animosity was so intense for each other that at one point it all just erupted; and in a moment of deep and rageful anger, the husband screamed, "You're disaffecting from me and I can't stand it."

That was it. There was nowhere else to go with all the anger after that. He'd touched his anger's deepest strata—vulnerability. He wasn't mad at his wife's behaviorist methods of child-rearing. Nor was he disgusted with her penchant for overspicing soufflés. No. He was enraged because he felt she was losing love for him.

Once he'd touched that deepest level of his rage, he could begin to feel all the emotional pain, the pain his anger had been covering up. Sitting in his chair, teary-eyed, he was no longer ranting and raving at his wife, but only experiencing his fears about her waning love. He was no longer repelling his wife with his vitriolic attacks; she could then walk over to him and try to comfort him. Their fight could end, in other words, once the deepest levels of his anger had been reached.

Fights, of course, don't always magically end this way. A man's simply reaching the point where he's experiencing his insecurities, not just his anger, doesn't guarantee that his wife or girlfriend will capitulate. What it does guarantee, though, are much better odds that if she wants to, she can make peace.

I watched another man argue with a woman he'd been living with for many years. During a lull in their heated fighting, the woman turned to me and soberly mentioned that perhaps it was her boyfriend's jealousy and his too-close ties to his family that were causing a lot of the problems in their relationship. Her statement, a reflective comment meant to be constructive and conciliatory, ignited her boyfriend. All of a sudden, he started verbally attacking her, dredging up every weakness he'd ever seen in her: Her too-fused relationship with an older sibling, her social awkwardness, her dependence on a therapist. It was very clear, by the suddenness and by the viciousness of his attack, that he was unable to reflect on the deeper issues she'd brought up—his jealousy and his close ties to his parents.

Most men use the Anger Demon to avoid looking at their own deepest emotional turmoils and vulnerabilities. It's simply a lot easier for a man to get angry at his wife or girlfriend than for him to try to understand himself and how he's contributing to his relationship's difficulties.

Women, too, use anger to avoid looking at themselves. This process, whereby we ignore our own inner tensions and blame everything on our spouses, is, therefore, rampant in intimate relationships.

Unfortunately, it's very hard to spot this blaming process as it operates in a relationship. It works very subtly. A friend of mine, for instance, was at a wedding. At this wedding, his wife began talking to a man. This man and my friend's wife—both of them passionate show-tune lovers—soon began singing the scores from *Oklahoma!* and *Carousel*. But after half an hour, my friend just couldn't contain his mounting feelings of jealousy any longer. Grabbing his wife, pushing her beyond the crowds, he finally lashed out at her for being excessively flirtatious.

His wife may have been flirtatious; perhaps even excessively so. But by reviling her for her flirtatiousness, he was also totally ignoring—in fact, not even mentioning—his own unmanageable feelings of jealousy: His torrents of abusive and self-righteous anger simply made it impossible for his wife to even mention his jealousy. (The psychological dynamics of the Jealousy Demon will be examined in greater depth in the following chapter.)

By excessively blaming our mates, we often end up avoiding looking at ourselves. In that process, we distort what's really wrong in our love relationships. It's always our mates who are at fault, always our mates who are petty or selfish or too dependent or not dependent enough.

Clearly, anger can be a way for a man to avoid dealing with his most frightening and bedrock emotional issues. But there's an even worse and, unfortunately, all too common avoidance mechanism men employ. They retreat. And they retreat not only from their softer and more vulnerable feelings but from their most intense feelings of anger, as well. As a result, they end up be-

coming emotionally detached, interpersonally withdrawn, and extremely passive in their romantic relationships.

Why do men opt for this sort of passive retreat? Because by becoming so emotionally withdrawn, they can
accomplish two things: They can avoid examining their
deepest torments and insecurities; and, by using this
withdrawing technique, they can transform their wives
into constant nags. A woman who's emotionally invested
in a remote man can do only one of two things: She can
either withdraw from her husband (as well as from her
own deepest self) or she can constantly pester her husband for some genuine display of emotion. In either
case, she loses, becoming either invisible or a nag.

Not surprisingly, many of the men I interviewed saw
themselves as the calm and sane partner in their romantic relationships, their wives or girlfriends, of course,
becoming the nonstop, hysterical complainers. "She's
always bitching about something" was the most frequent
complaint I heard about women from men. But again,
what most men didn't want to see was their contribution
to this transformation: That it was their own withdrawn
and passive styles that had made "complainers" of their
wives or girlfriends. As one woman, a fifty-two-year-old
nursery school teacher, confided:

> The real problem and the real reason why my rela-
> tionship with my husband had to change was that
> there was no relationship. There were no arguments
> but there needed to be arguments. . . . Arthur, like
> his mother, was very proud of the fact that people
> couldn't argue with him. He boasted about that. You
> couldn't pick an argument with him. He wanted to

hear no criticism, no violence, no anger. He'd say, "What's so bad? Why are you so unhappy? What's the matter? I'm a perfectly good husband. I support you, a lovely home, two-car garage, PTA, healthy children. What's wrong?" . . . So I became the crazy one while he just refused to look at anything.

Another woman, a sixty-four-year-old widow, had a similar story to tell:

> We quarreled a great deal. I say we quarreled an awful lot but with Victor you couldn't really quarrel. That was one of the very frustrating things about him: He was so closemouthed that the minute you tried to argue with him he'd withdraw or walk out. He just never showed any signs of anger. You know, you had to tear the walls apart before you got any response to your anger.

This sort of passive or nonengaged pose—this pose so many men use to cope with their intimate relationships—is, again, nothing more than a suppression of the Anger Demon. In their waking lives, these men have adopted this more remote or pseudo-cooperative stance toward their wives or girlfriends. But their fantasies, as well as their nightly dreams, are often filled with a ghoulish compendium of woman-hating and woman-maiming images. "Passivity," the writer William Lederer says, "is often a defense against aggression."

These remote men, beneath the surface, are sitting atop a keg of highly explosive and invariably misdirected anger at their mates. Who these men are really mad at is their parents and themselves. More than likely, they're mad at their parents for never having given them the emotional strength and confidence needed to sustain a genuinely intimate relationship. And they're mad at themselves because, deep down, they've glimpsed their own inadequacy and unhappiness.

\* \* \*

My own battles with this Anger Demon were fierce. I remember knocking down a door once, then grabbing Vivien and screaming at the top of my lungs till I nearly burst a vocal chord. Another time, banging my fist against a wall. Or Vivien, in an empty bathtub, sobbing hysterically, then breaking a vase and running out into a cold Maine night. Or just wretched weekends when we'd rage at one another, then sink into depressed pits; finally, pathetically pleading with each other for forgiveness.

To put it mildly, my fuses eight years ago, when I first met Vivien, all led back to a very volatile jungle of crisscrossed wires; a fairly common wiring schemata, I should add, for many men (especially men who get romantically involved in their early or midtwenties). At that age—if at any age—men just don't know who they are. They're strangers to their inner lives, still too raw and too molten. So a gentle criticism or challenge by their new wives or girlfriends about some seemingly small matter can too easily be misinterpreted by them as a smashing blow to their egos' still unsettled foundations.

Again, like many men, I knew very little about who I was when I first met my wife-to-be. As a result, something Vivien would say to me, and it could be something very innocuous, might kick off a full-fledged fight. It usually *was* something minor; maybe something about my being too cautious a driver or just her reminding me our car needed oil. But again, there was little differenti-ation for me during those early years between "minor" and "major" criticisms. Anything Vivien said to me back then could too easily become a cataclysmic insult in my warped ears. And once enraged, I'd immediately go right for her vulnerable psychological jugular, to those fragile parts of herself she'd once so trustingly shared with me. I didn't just fight dirty back then. No. I was out to psychologically maim; my viciousness was a function of my not wanting to look—head-on—at my own shaky depths.

What was happening to me in those early years was a very familiar pattern, one I later saw repeated in many men's lives: If a woman's not totally supportive of a man, especially when the man is first becoming vulnera-ble to the woman, he'll often start feeling shaky. And depending on his temperament, he'll then start feeling either more-hurt-than-angry or more-angry-than-hurt. I was from the more-angry-than-hurt school. Most men are.

I spent many nightmarish months in those rough seas of the Anger Demon, and way too much time languish-ing in its unproductive aftermath, depression. There was no shortage of anger for me either, fueled, as it was, by tankloads of my own emptiness and by a desperate and frightened unwillingness to look at those empty depths. Anger, moreover, had been the one emotion I'd been encouraged to express throughout my life. When I was a kid, I'd gotten the message (from football coaches, film directors, and cub scout leaders) that strong men got angry; and the more self-righteous that anger, the more manly. So as I ranted and raved at

Vivien those months, my manhood, I was convinced, was quadrupling.

Vivien, of course, contributed her own "craziness" to those early fights of ours. If I sometimes could get lost in too much self-righteous anger, she could sometimes provocatively invite it. She could, for instance, become overly upset with a small delay. This is a very common argument-provoking dynamic for couples. We might be on our way out the door, for example, when the phone would ring, the resulting delay unduly upsetting Vivien. Her frustration would then seek some release—that release, unfortunately, too often materializing into blaming me for life's happenstance. Or more idiosyncratic to Vivien (who's a very active person), she could sometimes become overly concerned with not stopping at any red lights when we were in a car. If I was driving, she'd want me to make all the lights or, second best, slowly roll toward a red traffic signal. But coming to a dead stop at a light was anathema to her occasionally too-frantic nervous system. Needless to say, it was the sort of irrational desire that didn't go over very well with someone who prided himself on being overly cautious at the wheel.

* * *

*Who can do what to whom?* Every squabble, every skirmish, every vase-smashing battle we ever had ultimately involved this question. *How can he tell me not to have friends over just because he's tired?* Or, *How can she insist we use my advance money for a winter vacation?*

The question always was: Whose needs are going to get met here? Will I have to yield and give in to what she wants? Or will my desires get top billing?

Like two power brokers, we had to do what every new

couple must do. We had to negotiate. We had to try to create a livable and workable relationship. "When people marry," Dr. Don Jackson states, "the first important action which takes place is the attempt of each spouse to determine the nature of the relationship; that is, each wants the system to be satisfying to himself, and would prefer to achieve this end without changing his already established behavioral pattern. Each wants the other partner to make the accommodations. . . . For this reason, almost all marriages—at least at first—have friction."

So there were times naturally when I compromised, when I surrendered to Vivien's desires without feeling as if some essential part of myself had been violated. And there were times she compromised. And there were other times when neither one of us could yield an inch. Those were the times when the Anger Demon threatened to capsize our new vessel.

One of the first really grisly battles Vivien and I had—and it's a very common first fight—involved other people. We were with a friend of Vivien's, a former college roommate. Vivien and this friend began reminiscing, both of them becoming more and more animated with each "remembrance of things past." But as the night progressed, I found myself feeling increasingly resentful. For one thing, I was being left out of the conversation and that, certainly, was contributing to my feelings. But even more provocative, I was seeing a part of Vivien that night I'd never seen before—a cackling, "girlie" part. And it was completely turning me off.

The fact that my emotion-inhibited male eyes were distorting joyful relating between two women friends into juvenile "girlie" behavior was just something I had no way of seeing that night. Nor could I see that I was inflicting onto Vivien the anger I was feeling at myself for not being able to enjoy the evening. No. All I knew that night was that I couldn't stand who Vivien was being with me and this friend.

When her friend finally left, I viciously attacked Vivien. I told her she was some sort of Jekyll and Hyde, that I'd never seen anyone act so differently just because another person was around. Partly, it was my jealousy that was making me so angry; seeing Vivien being playful with someone other than me wasn't easy. But even more combustible was this revulsion I was experiencing, this revulsion at what I was convinced was Vivien's too changeable personality.

Again, the hydraulics behind our first fight are known to many new couples. As a couple spends a lot of intense and isolated time together during the early stages of their relationship, they begin feeling more and more comfortable with one another. They start knowing what they can expect from each other. But then, integrating that sense of themselves as a couple into their old social networks often proves problematic.

It takes a couple a long time to understand that who they are when they're alone together is naturally going to be very different from who they are when they're around others. And it takes couples an even longer time to notice that *both* spouses change around others, not just one. It wasn't just Vivien who changed that night her college friend visited. I, too, changed. I became more withdrawn and more socially awkward.

Taking the previously isolated lover-lover "system"— which is often a safe cocoon of mutual self-discovery and sexual intimacy—into the world can clearly be a very rocky maneuver.

\* \* \*

Daniel Levinson (whose research in the field of adult developmental psychology inspired Gail Sheehy's *Passages,* as well as his own book, *Seasons of a Man's Life*) sees one of the tasks of a young man in his late teens and early twenties as learning "about his inner resources and vulnerabilities in relation to women, and about what they offer, demand, and withhold from him."

Levinson, however, like many professionals, knows that for most men, especially most young men, relationships aren't their primary focus. Their thrust is "more towards mastering the external world than towards exploring the self." And he knows, too, that for most men, and again especially for young men, love—that most elusive of words—is characterized by "impersonal pleasure seeking, macho power seeking or inhibition of passion and sexuality."

It's truly one of the great crises of our society, and of almost all societies, Dr. Levinson feels, that men have to choose and start a family before they know quite what it is they're up to. "Most young men," he states, "are not ready to make an enduring inner commitment to wife and family, and they are not capable of a highly loving, sexually free, and emotionally intimate relationship." They need, therefore, to learn about these relationships. As Dr. Herb Goldberg further points out: "Marriage is condoned and sometimes even encouraged for a man in his early twenties—long before he has had time to develop and grow emotionally, to leave adolescence, to define himself vocationally and philosophically, and to achieve a fairly secure economic foothold."

Instead of forming emotionally meaningful relationships, a lot of men (but again, especially young men) seek out women because they're in search of a sex object, or because they want to be narcissistically fed, or because they need a temporary maternal haven—some soft place to momentarily deposit their loneliness. Most men, simply, aren't looking for truly intimate, committed relationships.

The tragedy in our culture is that women too often fail to know this, blinded as they are by their own legitimate (but sometimes overwhelming) needs for nurturance: Most of the women I interviewed, therefore, wanted more from their relationships than men did. They were looking for something other than a hit-and-run type of relationship. They were looking for relationships that could touch and involve their personalities' deeper parts.

This naturally proved painful for many women because often the men they were involved with—some of these men because they were afraid, others because there were ignorant of the potential emotional depths of a romantic relationship—just couldn't give these women what they wanted. Indeed, too often, all these men could give to women was their pent-up rage and confusion.

\*　　\*　　\*

Ultimately, a man's inner emptiness is what makes him resort excessively to the Anger Demon. This inner emptiness, as I've already explained, is nothing other than a man's being out of touch with his emotions—with his feelings of tenderness, vulnerability, and compassion.

Now it's very difficult for a man to move beyond these

feelings of inner emptiness and into the more real and more vulnerable parts of himself. It requires a very special sort of journey, one generally involving a long and sometimes painful process of self-reflection.

In the earliest stages of a love relationship, a man doesn't really have to start on that journey. He can, for a while anyway, still get away with not having to operate from his more truthful and vulnerable depths. Because he's being appreciated and admired, and sometimes even idealized by a woman during these early stages of love, he's able to feel on top of things. There's no need for him to examine his harder-to-look-at layers.

Unfortunately, too many men just want to stop things at this point. They want to be adored by women. They want to be admired. Beyond that, though—beyond these initial flattering moves of a relationship and into the more vulnerable terrains any intimate relationship must enter—many men don't want to go. Many men, in fact, once they do get this sort of admiration from a woman, quickly lose interest in the relationship.

These men, filled either with an arrogantly inflated sense of their own "specialness," or else with a gnawing sense of their own inner emptiness, are unable to value anyone who genuinely values them. They end up, therefore, moving from one relationship to the next, callously disappointing several women in the process. Afraid there's no emotionally pulsating center in their beings, or else afraid that what *is* pulsating just below their 'pseudo-selves' is some grotesque cesspool of pent-up rage, obsessive sexuality, and infantile dependency, many men opt to let sleeping dogs lie. It almost seems better, they tell themselves, to live with a gnawing sense of emptiness than to start wrestling with long-buried demons: By rapidly pursuing a career, or else by some warped Holy Grail search for peak sexual experiences, or even by constantly and arrogantly invoking the Anger Demon, these men choose to never deal with their more vulnerable and initially more frightening depths.

Too many men, as a result, take from women what they can't give to themselves—a self-love, a genuine acceptance of themselves. And too many men are very adept at seductively eliciting this sort of admiration and respect from women. But in the end, if a man doesn't struggle to give this gift to himself, then his romantic relationships can only be short-lived and convulsive.

*   *   *

There's a word talk-show hosts, clergymen, and marriage counselors all love. It's a simple word, especially considering it's one of the few weapons we have against the Anger Demon. The word is *communication.*

*Communication.* During the past ten years, there has been a proliferation of marital therapies whose intent is to facilitate "communication" between embattled spouses. "Communication skills training," "fight fair workshops," "couples contracting workshops" have all been developed. Each of these psychological first-aid kits was designed to slow two people down so they could examine, in a more neutral and noninflammatory setting, their relationship's most volatile interactions.

These weekend workshops and short-term therapies are useful. I've met many couples who've been helped by them. Nevertheless, I feel a cautionary note is needed: All of us need to know that, bottom line, you can't rebuild a relationship—you can't learn how to "communicate"—in a single marathon therapy weekend. At best, you might be able to see how much hatred and anger actually exist between you and your spouse in one of these intensive couples weekends. You might even glimpse the love that's so long been absent from your relationship—which, no doubt, will create its own profound but ultimately short-lived euphoria. But as to restructuring a love relationship and learning how to communicate, these just aren't feats that are accomplished in two or three days. They're often slow, painstaking processes.

*     *     *

Vivien and I tried a number of these "communication" methods, these "fighting fair" techniques. We even devised some of our own. We once invented a game called "Tougee-Tougee." In the midst of a fight, if either one of us remembered to initiate the game, then both of us were bound, by a ceremonial handshake, to play it. The game consisted of the two of us tagging each other and then running around the house like spastics, all the while yelling the meaningless word "Tougee-Tougee." We were hoping that invoking this ridiculous game in the midst of an interminable battle, might derail some of our seemingly boundless rage.

The game often worked: If what we were fighting about wasn't terribly combustible, the game helped to dislodge our anger. But if things already had escalated to too volatile a place, "Tougee-Tougee" was useless.

There were other stratagems we concocted in our attempt to de-claw the Anger Demon. If we were on the verge of a fight, we agreed that one of us could leave the house (or wherever else we were fighting) for thirty minutes. After thirty minutes, we had to return home and talk about whatever precipitated the argument. We then had an hour to figure things out. If an hour passed and we still hadn't gotten anywhere, we'd drop the fight, each of us going our separate ways.

These rules all helped. They allowed us to cool down a bit so we could talk more sanely about our problems: We knew that if we could stop being venomous rivals, we had a better chance of settling our differences. If we could somehow stop blaming each other, at least we could start hearing what the other had to say.

But however useful these games and fighting rules proved, they were—ultimately—only secondary defenses in battling the Anger Demon. In our relationship, and in almost all romantic relationships, the major assault came—and must come—from a series of hard inner battles. These are the inner battles every man and every woman must wage within himself or herself. "There are no panaceas and no substitutes," Dr. Robert Seidenberg, the author of *Marriage Between Equals,* says, "for the work and agony involved in the confrontation of one's history." There's just no way around the difficult task of self-exploration. If what we're after are mutually satisfying romantic relationships, then each one of us needs to do his or her inner homework.

This "inner homework" is what allows a couple to fight fairly. It's what allows them to discern the real underlying issues behind a fight, thereby obviating debilitating surfacey tensions. And it's what allows them to be not defensive, but instead, able to hear what their mate is saying, even in the midst of a heated battle.

A number of the men I spoke to *had* looked beyond their anger and into their murkier parts. They were attempting to see how they contributed to the problems in their love relationships. But most of the men I interviewed wanted—at all costs—to avoid this sort of self-examination. They'd chosen, instead, anger as a powerful smokescreen. But by doing that, they'd also driven away the one thing they really wanted and needed in their lives: The love and caring of a woman.

\*　　\*　　\*

I have journals filled with indignant, outraged letters to Vivien, letters written in those unhinged moments after one of us either smashed the phone down or slammed the front door. Over the years, those letters have degenerated from thoughtful attempts at deciphering the complex vectors of our fights and fighting styles to the most outraged and crazed hate letters. It's sometimes just so easy to lose sight of why you're with the person you're with. There are too many years of resentments, too many years of recurring patterns, of constant frustrations and daily skirmishes.

Over the years, I've seen how hard it still is for me to let go of my anger once I feel I've been provoked by Vivien beyond certain limits. I'll become cynical, rageful—bleak about Vivien, about her ability to change, about our marriage in general. I'll see her, in those moments, as this hysterical ogress who's out of control, as this frantic whacko who's continually flooding our life with people I don't even care about; in the process, depriving me of my temperament's essential nutrient—reflective time, solitude.

I'll usually fail to see in those moments that my own unforgiveness, my own vengeful rampages on Vivien's self-esteem, are equally uncontrollable as her sometimes excessively social impulses. I'll forget, in other words, that our relationship is an interactional system—that the things I do affect her in similar ways. I'll end up seeing myself only as being victimized, defending myself from my wife's abuses—the only real course of action left to me.

At those times, I forget why we're married. And I forget we've helped each other through much worse times and that who we are today we owe, in large part, to one another. I forget, in other words, I've been at that hopeless state before and that love—in the guise of a close friend, a book, or sometimes just a simple gesture of Vivien's—has again and again made me reappreciate what we have; that love has freed me over and over again from the Anger Demon's bleak blinders.

I'm reminded in those moments of why I came together with this woman in the first place: I remember what Vivien and I share—an incredible ability to be real with one another and to be tender.

After a while, couples start to know their major areas of conflict. "Other Women" is what torments one couple I know. The man is continually fantasizing about what life would be like with another woman. Or "not enough emotional communication" is the nemesis of another couple I'm friendly with. ("Not enough emotional communication," by the way, is many couples' nemesis.) Or too much social activity followed by too much unforgiving rage is mine and Vivien's. The list is endless. But what isn't endless is the stamina of each marital combatant to keep on coming out on love's side after still yet another battle has blown over. What isn't endless, too, is the wisdomful counseling of friends and professionals. Only love is endless. What difference does that make, though, if you and your spouse have allowed the Anger Demon to wreck each other's receiving tuners—your hearts.

# CHAPTER FOUR

# THE JEALOUSY DEMON

IT'S A SADISTIC BEAST. It enjoys yanking out a man's teeth, one by one. I've often seen it destroy men, turning otherwise productive and gentle men into near homicidal maniacs. The Jealousy Demon, feeding as it does on a man's worst fears and most unexamined self-doubts, is an especially cruel obstacle on the road to love.

Some jealousy, of course, is a natural component of any love relationship. "The lover who is not jealous," the twelfth-century writer Capallanus said, "is not a true lover."

"Jealousy is an expected affect of living," Dr. Robert Seidenberg confirms. "If someone is precious to us, we must have a modicum of jealousy as basic cement."

But when this basic cement becomes a sinking weight that plummets a man deeper and deeper into the frightening waters of his own hostility, inadequacy, and fear, then it's no longer a tame part of love. Jealousy, at this point, starts becoming associated with paranoia and possessiveness. And, to use the vernacular, that's when it becomes a "bad trip."

I interviewed the twenty-eight-year-old owner of a movie house in Philadelphia. His recent and excruciating war with the Jealousy Demon had left him, he told me, a "shadow of my former self." "I was wasted by it," he said. "I was ruined. I lost weight. I was pale and shaky. I was constantly upset. And I didn't know how to get out of this state."

After a four-year involvement with a woman, he was—when I interviewed him—living alone again and "just trying to develop some inner confidence."

His story (included here almost in its entirety) very dramatically captures the psychological turmoil of the Jealousy Demon.

Our first year was fantastic. Fantastic communication. It was one of the only relationships I'd ever really wanted. It wasn't something casual in my mind. I wanted the relationship to last. I wanted us to stay together, to live together, to have a kid. The whole works. Those were my kinds of feelings. I began to feel for the first time that the whole thing—living with someone—could be something other than deadly.

So she was opening me up emotionally with all of our talking and communication. And I was opening her up sexually. That was just such an ego rush for me. She had been with other men but none of the sex had ever been good. She gave me insane confidence. At the time when I felt good with her, I was really bouncy and happy. I was just really letting myself go. But then, she started seeing this other man and I was just thrown into the pits. My ego was just slammed into the wall. I hid. I went away. I disappeared. I just stopped visiting people. I was tightening up. It was an incredible loss. I felt ashamed. When she started seeing someone else, I felt inadequate—inadequate in many ways. And I also felt that this guy she was seeing had a star personality and I didn't.

It all happened very fast. One night, she met a guy and I saw them go into her house together. And right away I was very upset. I wasn't used to seeing her with other people and I just reacted. I immediately said to her that she could do whatever she wanted to do. I was reacting more on what my value systems were. You know, I intellectually felt that it was OK for us to see other people. I felt, who was I to stop her from seeing others? Yet, in practicality, we were both monogamous. This was the first time it was actually questioned. So I reacted fairly OK that first night. But I reacted from my mind, not from what I was really feeling, which was just outrage, anger, frustration.

I remember I had to go away for a few days and when I returned, she came up to see me and told me that she saw Bob again and that they'd gone out to dinner and that they'd slept together. And I was just destroyed. She was telling me this because we'd always been honest with each other. She was just trying to be as casual and honest and as open as she could. I don't think there was any ill intent on her part. It was just like this-is-what-happened-and-I-have-to-tell-you. I immediately interpreted it that she was being so fucking callous. You know, I'm crushed, I'm trembling, and there I was inside a projection room of a movie theater, having to stand there for the next six hours showing movies. I was all alone. And being in that booth is like being in solitary. You know, in the best of conditions, being in a projection booth isn't the best place to spend six hours. But to be having this thing eating at me in that booth was too much.

I want to tell you, I was hurt. I was hurt because I felt I was inadequate, that I wasn't satisfying her. And I was very willing to criticize myself about that. I probably have a great innate tendency in that direction anyway. I was really hurt—my image, my self. And my work, owning a small movie theater, was becoming difficult at the time. The theater had money

problems and all. So I wasn't having any other satis-
factions in my life other than this relationship. The
relationship was my joy.

And this guy that Bonnie was with really hit me
hard. It was the sort of thing where I felt that I un-
derachieved but I felt that this person was really an
achiever. He's like a graduate of Cal Tech in physics
and he's got a master's in physics, and he was going
for his second master's in astronomy. He was an
achiever and I felt so out-classed. And another thing
that really hit hard was that she said she was going
down to the Caribbean with him, and I felt like,
"Wow, I can't do any of this stuff." First of all, I didn't
have the money. And I just felt so washed under.

I was very confrontational. I didn't know what to
do. I didn't know if I should like attack this guy, burn
his car, or get a samurai sword and come through his
window at night. And I did some of these weird
things, too. I came up to them in the middle of the
night when they were in bed together and I'd pound
on the door. I actually came sneaking up one night—
but they weren't there. I had this incredible vision of
somebody dying and I had a knife and it was just
lucky that no one was there. And I'd be walking
around the streets at four o'clock in the morning,
walking alone and feeling crushed. Just insane.

I finally told her I just couldn't see her anymore. It
was too painful for me to see her. I was real con-
fused. . . . I was really sick at heart when we left
each other, deeply sick about the whole thing. And I
just wasn't getting satisfied. My friends, other
women—nobody seemed able to satisfy me. There
was so much unhappiness. And then I'd feel that, you
know, life is too short. So I'd go back and see her. But
then I'd run away again. So I'd see her a little bit and

we'd go out a few times, but then, invariably we'd get into some conflict.

Finally, last February, I said to her that I've been doing this back-and-forth relationship long enough. Now I really have to walk away from it. There was still a lot of pain, and I said to her some really horrible things one night—that we never had a really good relationship, that we never talked to each other, that she was actually dishonest. And we both reacted very painfully and we ran away from each other. And I didn't see her for quite a while after that.

Then, I met her one day walking with Bob. And my reaction for a long time to this guy was like I just didn't want him in my sight. Anytime I'd ever be physically close to him, I'd just be in a tense posture. I mean, I felt quite willing to kill him. And that's a whole other thing—dealing with violent emotions like that. But finally I got to the place where I could look at him when he was with her and be able to say "hi." You know, that was pretty hard. It took me a long time to get to that.

I feel that now I'm in a process of sitting back and watching things. I'm working on myself. For a while I was just going after relationships and I didn't know what the hell I wanted. You know, I was knocking around in absurd ways and getting no satisfaction. Now I'm trying to come out of that and I'm starting to feel that the world is not this hustle, this difficult thing; that it's just there and it can be OK. I still feel pretty hurt and alone sometimes, but I think I'm ready to experience things again.

\*     \*     \*

Jealousy can obviously provoke a gauntlet of difficult feelings—anger, pain, a crisis of self-esteem. At its worst, as in the story you just read, it can precipitate an inner avalanche, a man's entire sense of himself caving in. These are very frightening feelings. Understandably, they can lead a man to taking desperate measures. A man in the throes of the Jealousy Demon needs something, anything, to regain a sense of himself.

To grab hold of some last shred of cohesiveness, men impaled on the razor-sharp horns of the Jealousy Demon will usually turn to one (or all) of the following: Violence, paranoia, or possessiveness.

In the case of the movie house owner, he'd resorted to violence in his worst moments of despair and inner disintegration. Another man I interviewed told me how he'd become a "CIA agent" because of jealousy. He was totally paranoid, thinking his wife was having an affair with a man she'd once briefly mentioned was attractive. This man began following his wife to work, listening to all her phone calls, incessantly interrogating her. And another man I spoke with, similarly caught on the fanged claws of the Jealousy Demon, had become utterly, maniacally possessive. He'd refused to let his wife out of their house. For two days, he barricaded her in a room. When the woman's brother finally freed her, this man was taken to a hospital for psychiatric observation.

Why is it that jealousy mildly irks some men while it savagely destroys others? Why can some couples even use it as a way to get their relationship out of a boring phase—as a way to re-kindle interest in one another— while other couples are consumed by even a small dosage?

Simply stated, it's a man's degree of insecurity that's the determinant to how much jealousy he (and, therefore, any relationship he's in) can tolerate. A very insecure man will crumble at the slightest glimmer that his wife is interested in another man. He may even paranoically concoct that glimmer, if he's that dependent on his wife. I've seen men become irrationally enraged at their girlfriends or at their spouses for talking just a little too long to another man—even if that man was a close friend or relative.

Insecure men are utterly unhinged by this demon because at some very primal level, they sense that their wives are all they have. With little meaning in their work lives and with generally estranged relationships with friends and fellow workers, these men are nearly totally dependent on their wives—dependent on them for a sense of inner security. Understandably, if someone shows even the remotest signs of affection for their wives (may it be a man or a woman), these men immediately become wary.

Jealousy, as Margaret Mead observed, "is not a barometer by which depth of love can be read; it merely records the degree of the lover's insecurity."

\*　　\*　　\*

The movie house owner felt threatened by his girlfriend's new lover. He felt "outclassed," overwhelmed by a feeling of inadequacy when he compared himself to this new man. These feelings of inadequacy are part of any man's wretched bout with jealousy.

My own battles were typical. Two years after Vivien and I met, we decided to get married. We were married on May 29, 1977, a warm May afternoon. As part of our wedding celebration that day, we rented a movie theater and showed to our guests Frank Capra's *It's a Wonderful*

*Life.** That movie's message, very briefly, is how precious one person's life can be to the people around them. It was the message we wanted to affirm in our marriage.

After our marriage, our lives became very busy. Vivien returned to graduate school, and I began writing screenplays. As a result, with very little time for each other, things felt rocky those first months of marriage.

Rocky, but still manageable. But then, when Vivien developed an attraction for a teacher of hers at school, our precarious stability exploded. And that was when my nightly dreams exclusively started running horror films.

That month-long horror festival ran a different dream-movie every night, each dream having more or less the same plot: I'd be playing with a loose tooth in all these nightmares and that tooth would fall out. Next, there'd be this horrid collapse of my dental structure, not only my teeth but all my gums caving in—my mouth becoming a chaotic, frightening void. In their uncanny symbolic language, I knew these dreams were trying to tell me something: That Vivien's infatuation was caving in any sense I had of myself. I was disintegrating.

I didn't need my dreams to tell me that, though. In my waking life, I was equally anxious and paranoid. I remember standing by our bedroom's closed door whenever Vivien would be on the phone, frantically trying to listen to every call she made; or else eavesdrop-

---

*Jimmy Stewart starred in this 1948 classic about a would-be suicide who's saved by an elderly angel. The angel shows Jimmy Stewart, who plays a small town businessman, how deeply he would have been missed by his friends and family had he not lived.

ping whenever a friend of hers visited; or always desperately trying to diminish this teacher of hers whenever she mentioned something he'd said or demonstrated in class. (Because I'd never met him, though, finding his weak points proved no easy task. If I said he was just another teacher on a power trip—his students the easy audience he'd been craving all his life—Vivien would casually dismiss my observations, telling me I wasn't being fair to him, especially since I'd never even met him. And I knew she was right. There really wasn't anything—either positive or negative—I could say about him. Except that I hated him.)

This teacher of hers became an ever-present "leading man" in my dreams. In these dreams, he would be a dynamic, strong, inspired, and inspiring man, every moment of his life filled with some challenging work or with a deep human interchange. He even slept only a couple of hours a night, that's how alive my unconscious was painting him. Best of all (worst of all for me), not a single moment of his existence was ever tainted with any depression. He was truly awesome.

As the painful weeks became painful months, this dynamic man was destroying me. Again, my work felt insignificant next to his. My relationships, by comparison, all superficial. It really felt as if every moment of my life were either being haunted at the center or on the peripheries by this spectral lover of hers: Just the thought of him made him loom so large on my inner landscape that any sense I had of myself quickly disintegrated.

I paranoically assumed that to share all these insecurities with Vivien would only push her deeper into a relationship with this teacher. Why would she want to be with someone as "untogether" as me, when she could be with this perfect specimen? Why a twerp, when Dynamic Man was waiting in the wings?

Eventually, my emotions became too obsessive for me to handle alone. I just couldn't play the nonchalant, together husband anymore. With my teeth falling out in my dreams every night, and with my every waking moment haunted by this teacher, there was just no way to maintain a protective, silent pose.

I ended up telling Vivien everything. I told her about all the self-doubts I was being tormented by, about my nightmarish dreams, my fears of losing her. And she responded with great love. She tried to reassure me. She held me. She made love to me. But her reassurances just couldn't penetrate my paranoia-blocked ears: The more she told me she loved me, the more I doubted it. The more she reassured me there was nothing going on between her and this teacher, the more certain I was they'd already passionately embraced.

I must have shared those swirls of inner chaos with my new wife twenty or thirty times, until finally I started sensing the futility of telling her soberly or, as was more frequently the case, histrionically and desperately, about them. I just started seeing that it wasn't going to work: As much as I wanted Vivien to ease my pain, as much as I wanted her to magically make it all go away, as much as I even wanted her to feel responsible for my pain, I just knew, at some deeper place, that this was one demon I was going to be battling alone.

\*     \*     \*

My dreams had shown me jealousy's horror show. They were now going to show me a way out.

During the next few months, there were other men

whom Vivien found either attractive, energetic, or talented. The world, fortunately or unfortunately, is filled with alluring men and exciting women. But now I was starting to see something: Each time Vivien innocently told me about some interesting man, I'd immediately bloat him way out of proportion in my dreams. In dream after wretched dream, he'd become some kind of Superman; and simultaneously, I'd deflate myself into the most ineffectual of men. These men would become vital, attractive, and charismatic in these dreams, while I'd be some sort of pathetic nebbish.

It didn't take any genius on my part to realize that these dynamic men, these men who were nightly starring in my dreams, weren't the men Vivien was attracted to. Rather, these dream-men were fantastic, idealized versions of myself. Everything I doubted about myself—how dynamic I was, how attractive I was, how I needed too much sleep—simply became the building blocks my unconscious would use to assemble these larger-than-life dynamos. My unconscious was painting these men larger than life, using my private palette of insecurities for paint.

Discerning my deepest insecurities amidst these nightly Dynamic Men collages helped pry me from the Jealousy Demon's claws. Seeing that the cartilage, the flesh and blood, of this demon was nothing less and nothing more than my own worst fears and most unexamined self-doubts made the Jealousy Demon much less frightening: At that point, jealousy started feeling less like some foreign invader and more like an inner dynamic I could observe.

Later on, as these wretched bouts with jealousy subsided, my dreams, interestingly, started taking a positive turn. I still had dreams where I'd lose a tooth. But what stopped happening was that horrid avalanche of all thirty-two. One tooth would fall out; but now I could study it, observe its cavities, even analyze the possible causes of decay. Extending the dream metaphor, no longer was my entire sense of myself collapsing when I became jealous. Some part of me, like a periscope capable of seeing over the emotional torrents—over jealousy's tidal waves—had finally been established. And much later on—when jealousy was a normal rather than a *demon*-ic component of my love for Vivien—I started having what I'll call my "All-American" dream series. I'd be smiling in these dreams, a near perfect set of solid white teeth securely set in my gums.

*     *     *

Men aren't only jealous of other men. Oftentimes, they're jealous of their wives' or girlfriends' women friends, as well. Jealousy doesn't discriminate between the sexes.

Possibly because Vivien had been an only child, she'd developed, over the years, a network of very close women friends. They were like sisters. (These intense friendships of hers were naturally a revelation to me. By comparison, my own friendships with men seemed so superficial—tame, competitive note-swapping sessions really. So as much as I sometimes hated these friendships of Vivien's, as much as I, later on, became maniacally jealous of them, I couldn't help but also respect them, even their seeming excesses—the marathon phone calls, the wild laughter, the tears.)

Phone calls would come in from all parts of the country—New York City, Los Angeles, San Francisco. At two in the morning, there'd be a call, another waking me up a few hours later. And each time the phone would ring, Vivien would jump out of our bed and grab the phone. For the next hour or so, I'd have to listen to unbounded laughter and shrieking from behind our bedroom's closed door.

One of these close friends felt especially abandoned by Vivien when Vivien and I started living together. This woman was living with a man. But men, I was bluntly told, didn't really count. *You needed them but they could never supply you with enough emotional intensity.* Men come and go, I was to understand. It's your women friends who are permanent.

Over the years, as these women have made deeper connections with men and as I've slowly befriended the Jealousy Demon, my jealousy toward each of them, as well as their jealousy toward me, has all but disappeared. But even now, when one of them calls on a Sunday morning—when Vivien and I are lounging in bed—I can still feel jealousy's quills, as Vivien gleefully rushes for the phone.

The Jealousy Demon dies hard.

\* \* \*

Intense jealousy is nothing less than a plea from a man's deepest self to look at his darkest pockets of self-denigration, as well as at his deepest uncertainties about his desirability to women. When the Jealousy Demon strikes, it's time for a man to radically and honestly re-evaluate himself.

For a man, making peace with the Jealousy Demon means nothing less than making peace with his most despised short-comings and his most fragile insecurities.

# CHAPTER FIVE

# THE TIME DEMON

THE EXTINCTION Demon, the Fusion Demon, the Anger Demon, and the Jealousy Demon are typically demons who live in the early stages of a love relationship, each of them, as I've already shown, thriving in the undernourished soils of a man's inner emotional emptiness. But as a man and a woman negotiate their relationship—as they begin to figure out some of its complexities—these demons will usually lose some of their original strength. One demon, though, the Time Demon, unlike any of these other demons, becomes more and more treacherous as a relationship ages.

This Time Demon isn't as flashy as any of the other demons. It works much more like slowly corroding rust than a bolt of rageful or jealous lightning. But it's as potent as any of these other demons, and probably destroys more relationships.

After a few years of marriage, a lot of couples think they can put their marriages on some kind of automatic pilot. Husbands especially feel they can leave their "solid" marriages on hold, and then attend to what really needs tending to—their careers, their self-growth, their childrens' educations, their five-year economic plans. But I've seen too many marriages too quickly nose-dive once this sort of automatic pilot's thrown into gear.

Typically, at the beginning of a relationship, both partners want to spend a lot of time together. "The urge for great amounts of togetherness," says Dr. Don Jackson, "is par for the course in the courtship phase of a relationship." This is when two people are first discovering each other. It's when the thrill of their mutual appreciation is so electric. But these initial jolts of ego-affirming electricity inevitably de-intensify. And nine out of ten times it's men who first experience this de-intensification and who then return to the workaday world.

"A man spends a lot of time with a woman in courtship," says Dr. Jackson. "But afterwards, he devotes a lot of time to his work, telling his wife it's for their mutual welfare. But that's a shift that needs to be worked out."

So men, in the course of a love relationship, tend to shift their primary focus from their wives to their work. It's an understandable shift: Considering the economic responsibilities all of us have to meet, coupled with the fact that we all derive so much of our self-esteem and self-worth from our work, it isn't only understandable, it's logical. But what isn't logical is that so many men, at some point in their relationships, *totally* lose interest in their wives or girlfriends.

How is this possible? How can men who once loved being with their wives end up totally neglecting them?

A thirty-four-year-old lawyer from Chicago spoke to me about his battles with the Time Demon. His comments help answer this question:

> When Denise and I first met, I just wanted to be with her all the time. We'd hang out in bed all day. It was an effort to even get out of bed for food. But after a while, I just didn't feel like it was enough.
>
> Friends of mine were telling me how they'd just

scored fifty-thou on some fast real estate deal; and another friend was a big-wig producer in Hollywood. I just felt if I didn't make my move, I'd be left behind.

That's when I started putting in fifteen-hour days at the office . . . I remember driving home one night. I was really exhausted. When I finally pulled my car into the driveway, I just fell asleep. The next morning, I ran into the house, brushed my teeth, and drove right back to work.

I thought our relationship could handle that sort of stuff. But one night, I came home and Denise had written me this long note. Basically, she said if I didn't cool it, she wanted out.

I couldn't stop, though. It was like this thing was over my head. I felt this pressure to perform, to be recognized. Maybe it's a cultural thing, I don't know. Or maybe it has something to do with my family; being the youngest son, I wanted to show my father I could make it big in the world.

When Denise finally left, I was making about eighty-thou a year; and that's a hot-shot lawyer by most people's standards. But now its like—what's the difference if I make thirty-five or seventy-five a year? I'm telling you, I really thought that was the most important thing—making money, being recognized. And I guess it is. Worldly accomplishments make a big difference. Just not when they're at the expense of your closest relationship.

This lawyer's relationship, like many men's relationships, suffered from an unchecked careerism: He couldn't keep his work life and his love life balanced.

It's a classic dilemma, especially for men who are in their late twenties and thirties. This is the time when a man is trying to gain some economic foothold in the world, when his deepest ambitious urges are sprinting toward whatever finish line he's set for himself. It's difficult for a man at this stage of his life to tame these wild horses of ambition.

For some men, the finish line they set for themselves is strictly monetary. They want to be earning a certain amount of money by the time they're, say, in their mid-forties. For other men, their finish line is winning a prestigious award, or a research grant, or a well-endowed teaching chair. For still other men, their goal is buying a summer cottage near the ocean or an antique sports car. Whatever a man's dream, it's generally during his twenties and thirties that he's most intensely going after it.

The fact that this is also the stage of life when many men are now choosing to get married has made this Time Demon treacherous. The balancing act between career and marriage has always been problematic. But today, with so many men marrying for the first time in their late twenties and thirties, this demon has become nothing less than ferocious. And, unfortunately, as case history after case history reveals, a man's love life, not his career, suffers most when this career/marriage balance is toppled.

\*     \*     \*

A man's inner life is filled with what I call "self-esteem spot checks." In their inner monologues with themselves, as well as in their conversations with others, men will frequently assess what they've attained (or what they haven't yet attained) in their lives. A research psychologist, for example, will talk to both himself and to others about the professional journals he's had articles in; a documentary filmmaker, about the awards he's garnered. To varying degrees, men will tell their wives, their friends, or themselves about the progress they're making toward their life goals. This inner tally sheet then very often determines how buoyant or how depressed a man feels about himself.

In moderation, these self-esteem spot checks are useful. They can help a man stay on course, to not waver from what he's decided are his realistic goals. But, too often, what happens is that these spot checks wind up becoming compulsive: Men, at this point, are more like shopkeepers who have to take complete inventories after every item they sell. They become compulsive careerists, their sense of well-being completely dependent on the daily fluctuations of their careers.

These spot checks—once gentle and useful reminders to stay on some chosen course—can just too quickly end up becoming driven and perfectionistic inner voices, voices blindly fueling a man's workaholism and careerism. It's at this point that love relationships are most susceptible to the Time Demon.

To some degree, almost all the men I interviewed for this book suffered from careerism. Living in our society, it's hard to avoid. Ours is a culture, as any copy of *People* magazine instantly makes clear, that glorifies success. It's very difficult, therefore, for a man to maintain his marriage as a priority in our culture. Again, the pull toward worldly success is just too fierce: Bottom line, it's material success, and not marital bliss, that all of us, as a society, encourage and reward. This shift from marriage to career, then, is practically unavoidable. But what can be avoided, and what every marriage needs to avoid, is having that shift run amuck.

\* \* \*

There's one way to ensure a marriage against the potential damages of the Time Demon, and that's by paying attention to it. Very simply, if you *don't* pay attention to your relationship, if you're constantly preoccupied, say, with a career, you just may not have a relationship after a while.

One of the major tasks in any marriage, therefore, is to pay attention to it. But the task happens to be one of the hardest because it involves consciously putting aside time, each day or each week, to do that. One couple, in their mid-fifties, after nearly succumbing to this demon, finally learned this truism: Namely, that marriage partners need to make time for their marriages.

JONATHAN: Over the course of our marriage, I'd get really involved in some work-related project and really excited about it. And if Claire wasn't involved, I'd kind of lose interest in her. At those times, I'd feel that the relationship wasn't that important and I'd take it for granted. And then home would just be a place to come back to to change clothes. But because of her strength, Claire's always brought me back to re-appreciating what we have.

CLAIRE: During these various crises, I'd make us talk more seriously about the two of us spending more time together. Every summer on vacation we'd make these great plans, these vows that next year we weren't going to get so busy, that we were going to spend more time going out to dinner, to plays, things like that. Then, on our vacation the following year, we'd end up saying the same thing.

At a certain point, I think you just have to grab hold of the reins of your marriage. Otherwise, it'll get away from you.

Marriages can wither away from emotional neglect. A genuine effort of the will is needed to prevent this from happening. Otherwise, the insidious Time Demon will undermine even the strongest of marital bonds.

*　　*　　*

For Vivien and me, it was a combination of careerism and a hyperactive social life that was robbing our marriage of the alone time it needed. For a long time, Vivien tactfully kept in the wings a major personality trait of hers: Her intense gregariousness. But when she started reconnecting to all her old friends—friends she'd only temporarily put on hold during our courtship—it was clear to me just how social she really was.

I was much more reclusive. I wanted our relationship to be a milder but still very insulated version of our first (though too-fused) months together. . . . Vivien was "Zippy" and I was "Zombie," one friend dubbed us. She wanted to zip around in the world; I wanted us to zombie-out at home. For Zombie, it felt as if our house was being invaded if more than three people visited on a weekend. For Zippy, three or four people meant the party was just starting.

Looking back, it was truly insane for this introvert—who for kicks sometimes just listened to the hum of his fluorescent desk lamp—to be living with a woman whose social calendar was as jam-packed with names as David Rockefeller's Rolodex.

To avoid fighting, I initially went along with Vivien's nonstop social life. Four or five nights a week, I trudged to dinner parties, picnics, and barbecues. But two things quickly started to happen: I began feeling resentful because Vivien was dictating our social life, and even more resentful because we were spending so little time together.

It all hit the proverbial fan in the third year of our marriage. We were at a lake one weekend, two other couples with us. Both these couples were close friends: All of us had seen, in other words, each other's "off-the-wall" sides.

There was a lot of tension between Vivien and me that day and it was coming out in all the small ways domestic tension seeps out before it's ready to explode. We were bickering about everything: What food we'd buy for the picnic, what type of gas to put into the car, where to park.

Finally, push came to shove; and if our friends hadn't seen, or else had politely ignored our subtle jabs, they could now no longer avoid our out-and-out shouting.

"What's going on with you two anyway?" one friend finally blurted.

"I don't want to get into it," I said. But I knew at that moment I wanted nothing more than to spend the next five hours getting into every last bit of it.

My rage, my resentments—resentments that had been building for months—exploded; bitter resentments that had marinated too long in the heated spittle of the Time Demon's mouth. Zippy's social excesses naturally were the focus for my rage—the seemingly never-ending potluck parties for eight, the crowds of friends who always accompanied us to the movies, the droves of weekend visitors. Vivien, in turn, blamed my work—my trips to Los Angeles and New York—for the little time we spent together.

"It's over. The whole thing," I screamed. I hadn't

threatened to leave her ever since our worst bouts with the Anger Demon.

"It's your fault," she yelled back, sobbing hysterically.

One of our friends, Jeff, quickly intervened. "Work out a schedule," he said. "Block out time each week for your work, your friends, yourselves, and, most of all, for your relationship."

*Time-Structured Therapy* (TST) was born at that moment. The name was playful, Jeff's caricature of est and all the other change-your-life-in-a-weekend regimens. But jokes aside, TST was our tentative truce, the speck of hope that finally allowed us to stop fighting that day.

\*     \*     \*

We initially rebelled at the idea of a schedule. We didn't want to regiment our lives. It seemed childish really, to have to block out specific hours during the week to be together or to see friends. But we couldn't stop fighting. So with our friends facilitating, we agreed to hammer out a schedule.

Predictably, I wanted more time with Vivien than she with me; and she naturally wanted more hours to socialize. Zippy and Zombie at Yalta. But after three agonizing hours at the bargaining table, a schedule we could both agree upon was signed by Vivien, me, and our two witnesses, Jeff and his wife.

It was a little awkward at first implementing the schedule. We needed some time to get used to the loss of spontaneity any schedule imposes. Having your life so compartmentalized feels a little strange initially. But within two weeks, the schedule started feeling OK. And within five weeks, I could no longer remember what my chaotic pre-schedule life had been like.

\*     \*     \*

TST seems simple. And it is. But its effects are profound. By structuring into a week inviolable islands of time for couples to be together—hours with none of the usual intruders (phones, friends, TV, kids)—relationships instantly start changing.

Vivien and I called our hours together "lock-ins." These hours were our marriage's sabbath; hours off the busy wheel of daily life. And what we quickly discovered was that we could unwind together during these lock-ins. We could begin to move beyond all the consuming and enervating superficialities of a shared life. *Did you do the laundry? . . . Where's the plumber's phone number? . . . Do we need more milk?* By having these chunks of uninterrupted hours together, we could talk about things other than diurnal logistics.

What happens in most marriages is there's barely enough time—because people don't make that time—to be together, especially in any meaningful way. Most couples, according to several recent surveys, spend less than *thirty minutes a day* together. And in thirty minutes (those thirty minutes usually coming after a depleting day of work and child care), it's just about impossible to intimately re-connect to your mate.

Real intimacy requires time, time that couples need to set aside for themselves. They need to share at least some of the small bruises all of us incur during any given day—those petty resentments we all feel toward our bosses, our kids, our auto mechanics, *and* toward our spouses.

Once those daily concerns, those inevitable bruises, are shared and filed away, spouses can then begin sharing more long-range preoccupations and dreams. And beyond that—beyond all those daily and not-so-daily concerns—they can start enjoying other and richer levels of intimacy—love-making, affectionate baby talk, unfettered play.

But again, what happens in too many relationships is that there's barely enough time to work through even that first batch of daily bruises. Should it come as any surprise, then, when many years later, a couple is asking themselves in a therapist's office, "Where did our love go?"—a love that was there for them when they used to spend every extra moment together at the beginning of their relationship?

\*　　\*　　\*

The "thrill," the excitement of being together, waxes and wanes in the course of any long-term relationship. Marriages, moreover, periodically gravitate to emotional nadirs, times when neither spouse is particularly interested in spending time with the other. But by locking in pockets of time, a couple can at least give their relationship the chance it needs to recover from one of these low points.

The demands of any given day—earning a living, cooking, taking care of children, mowing the lawn, socializing—rob a marriage of the hours it needs. Without that time together, though, too many spouses drift apart.

If a relationship doesn't periodically give itself time to soar, if it doesn't put aside time each day or each week to re-experience some of its magic—its tenderness, its laughter, its sexual excitement—then all the unavoidable and petty resentments any relationship daily manufactures will start festering. And eventually, these otherwise trivial resentments will undermine even the strongest of marriages.

# CHAPTER SIX

# THE
# LUST
# DEMON

HANDSOMELY AND POWERFULLY built, David recently had completed a graduate degree in engineering. At age thirty, and after two years of marriage, he was about to start his professional life. When I interviewed him, he was happy his student days were ending. But he was also a little scared to be entering—for the first time really—the nine-to-five world.

At a graduation celebration, he started talking to a woman he'd gone through three years of school with. She was one of the eight women in his class of ninety engineering students. Over the years, they'd flirted occasionally in study groups and at parties. There'd always been, David knew (and he surmised the woman knew), a sexual charge between them. In the three years they'd been in the program, however, they'd managed to ventilate the heat of that sexual charge by "flirting it away."

But for three weeks prior to this graduation celebration, David had started to become obsessed with this woman. He'd spent hours fantasizing about her, sometimes masturbating, he told me, as much as four or five times a day.

His vivid masturbation fantasies were always the same. In these fantasies, he'd be talking to her at a public place—a bar, a party, a classroom. Next, they'd give each other some sort of nonverbal message, both of them then leaving the room together. Finally, the minute they were back at her house—the moment the door was unlocked—they'd be ripping off each other's clothes.

At the graduation celebration—a party given by one of their professors—David began talking to this woman. He couldn't remember what they spoke about; but after twenty minutes, they excused themselves from the party. . . . The minute they were back at her house— the moment the door was unlocked—their clothes were unzipped.

It was the first time David committed adultery. And it came, as most adulterous episodes do, at a difficult time in his young marriage. His wife, Karen, in the midst of finishing her first year of social work school, was overwhelmed with work—writing papers, seeing clients, meeting her supervisors.

It would be very neat and compact if I could say that Karen's emotional unavailability led to David's affair. This is, of course, sometimes the case: As spouses emotionally and physically drift apart—as the Time Demon, in other words, insidiously creeps up on a couple—this Lust Demon often flourishes. But in David and Karen's situation, Karen—despite her busy schedule—was always available to David, offering him the support and affirmation he needed during his difficult life transition.

His affair wasn't triggered by the Time Demon. Rather, it was the result of a very deep-rooted and personal torment. He loved his wife. But he just couldn't reconcile himself to never again sleeping with a new woman.

\*     \*     \*

David had always been very physically attractive. In high school and college, he'd slept with dozens of admiring women. His physical attractiveness was a cornerstone upon which a lot of his self-esteem relied. So even after he and Karen had met, he'd managed to convince Karen to sexually experiment by adding a third partner to their love-making. On two occasions, Karen tried this arrangement. But she'd found it (unfortunately for David) not especially to her liking. She was, she knew, essentially monogamous.

David was hoping that by having an occasional *ménage à trois,* he could satisfy his strong sexual desires and not have to jeopardize his marriage: If he could occasionally share a new lover with Karen, he wouldn't have to seek out clandestine extramarital affairs.

His strong sexual curiosity, coupled with the fact that he'd been on the verge of entering the work world and seriously doubting his abilities to make it "out there," had led David to his extramarital affair. It was, simply, a very vulnerable time in his life and he needed to feel he was still an attractive and desirable man, not just a shaky and fledgling engineer.

\*   \*   \*

To have an affair or not to have an affair? It's a question every married man must wrestle with. And since men, as a rule, experience the sexual potential in many of their encounters with the opposite sex, the question is an ever-present one. The Lust Demon, in other words, accompanies men from adolescence to old age.

Men usually have some part of their attention attuned to the sexual possibilities, to the sexual desirability, of any woman they're with. It's sort of a low-grade universal male obsession. Women, on the other hand, usually don't experience this sexual attunement quite to the degree men do. Women aren't *always* "checking out" men, at least not with the sort of exclusively sexual radar men use. The Lust Demon, therefore, while often visiting a woman's life, tends (at least at some point) to plague a man's.

Is it normal for a man to be monogamous, or is it normal for a man to have an affair? Is there some biologically ingrained instinct in men for promiscuity? These are the questions that often get addressed when this topic of marital fidelity is discussed. But what rarely gets addressed is a much more fundamental question: How can a marriage deal with this inevitable demon?

Given the fact that all of us—men and women alike—have sexual feelings for people other than our mates, answering this question seems essential. If a marriage is to stay afloat in the often choppy waters of this demon, it needs clear-cut directives. Theoretical speculations as to whether or not male promiscuity is a biologically ingrained instinct can wait.

How to make peace with the Lust Demon—with this desire we all have to know people of the opposite sex—becomes the crucial question. How to make peace with this demon without hiding from it, or running away from it, or lying about it?

It's a very difficult question to answer in any marriage. But an answer does exist. There is a preventive to this demon. But unfortunately, most people just aren't willing to try it.

\* \* \*

There's no denying the thrill of a spontaneous, non-obligating sexual liaison. If we knew we could have intense affairs and one-night stands (and feel OK about our spouses having similar experiences), our sex lives would all be more variegated and probably filled with more moments of sexual abandon. "The revitalizing impact of a new sex partner," says Dr. Herb Goldberg, "is widely accepted. Many so-called impotent, passive, or disinterested men find themselves extremely potent with a new partner."

But also there's no denying the deep and upsetting emotions a marital partner's infidelity elicits in his or her mate. Anger, insecurity, and feelings of rejection all are evinced. "There is nothing so devastating," Dr. Allen Wheelis, a psychiatrist, states, "as finding out that the person you are in love with has betrayed you or lied to you."

It's always a choice, therefore, between the sizzling moment versus the painful aftermath whenever adultery is being contemplated.

This point seems obvious. Yet so many of the people I interviewed for this book missed this very obvious fact, and for a good reason: If you can manage to minimize, deny, or trivialize the pain you'll be inflicting on your spouse by having an affair, then it will be that much easier to have one. If you can somehow cleverly delude yourself into believing that having an affair won't really hurt your husband or your wife, then you're apt to have a much less guilt-ridden time.

\* \* \*

There are, I've observed, two ways men on the verge of having affairs gloss over their wives' inevitable pain. They either tell themselves that having an affair has nothing to do with their wives—that it has absolutely no connection to what they're feeling about their marriages—or they vow never to tell their wives.

In the Anger Demon section of this book, I presented

an interview with a Los Angeles theatrical agent. The second portion of my interview with him was about his extramarital affairs. Because it very much exemplifies how men delude themselves into thinking their affairs have little, if any, relationship to their marriages, I've included it here. His marriage, as you may recall, clearly was nose-diving:

My relationship with my wife has nothing to do with my extramarital affairs. See, if you're with a woman because the home scene is bad, then you're doing something else. I'm not looking for other women as a way of getting back at my wife. I don't see that it affects her at all. And this is all relatively new to me. I was absolutely faithful for seven or eight years. I never even kissed another woman. I didn't use to think that you could have both a marriage and outside affairs. I just thought that was the way marriage was. But, you know, things happen.

So whatever problems we've had in our marriage, and God knows there's been plenty, they've had nothing to do with my outside relationships. There are simply various pressures on our relationship that are caused by the fact that two intelligent people came together at the age of twenty-five or twenty-six and now it's fourteen years later. And they've both grown and developed and changed and had children and have gone through a lot of history on the way. That's what causes pressures.

I'm really not very sexually active outside my marriage. I would guess that if you took a survey of all the males who are married, I would end up in the bottom 10 percent in terms of the number of times I've had extramarital relationships. I mean, I know married guys who go out casually every night with other women.

This man refused to see that his affairs were even partially triggered by the unhappiness and frustation he was experiencing in his marriage. Many men I interviewed were similarly deluded. Tom, a thirty-five-year-old lawyer, told me this story.

A couple of years ago, I became involved with several women. One of the women was even the wife of a client of mine. I was married at the time—still am—so I thought I'd be tactful and not tell my wife. Why lay a trip on her? My wife didn't know any of the women. What would telling her about all my sexploits accomplish anyway?

What ended up happening was pretty classic. My wife found a letter at my office one day, a too-intimate letter from one of these women. And that was it. The cat was out of the bag.

Before all my affairs, we had a stillborn. We had one son. But Cheryl really wanted a girl this time. It wiped us both out. . . . We then tried to get pregnant as soon as we could but it just wasn't happening. Now I don't know if you know what that's like, trying to get pregnant and it not working. It's physically exhausting, for one thing. You begin to feel like you're a sex machine who has to perform at the drop of a hat. It takes the sex out of sex.

We went to a therapist because things were getting pretty ragged at home. The therapist encouraged us to hang in there. But I knew I wasn't feeling good being at home anymore.

We went back to this same therapist a few weeks

after my wife discovered my affairs and a lot of stuff came out. Besides us not getting pregnant, I was starting to feel my age a little. I was balding. Now that's something men don't like to talk much about. You know, they say, "Look how virile a guy like Telly Savalas is." Well, that's a crock. When clumps of your hair fall out, it really puts you through a heavy.

So the affairs didn't come from nowhere. When I first got into being unfaithful, I really didn't put two and two together. But talking to the therapist showed me why I was doing what I was doing.

Like this lawyer, a lot of men mentioned to me that it was necessary to be "tactful" in a relationship. By tactful, they meant it was better to conceal their affairs from their wives. *Why burden my wife with something that essentially has nothing to do with her or with our relationship?*

What these men didn't know, though, and what the Lust Demon preferred them not to know, was that ninety-nine out of a hundred times, an affair is an emotional barometer for a marriage: It's an indicator of what's going on between a husband and his wife. It's no coincidence, for example, that the theatrical agent's extramarital affairs began when his marriage started feeling rocky or that the lawyer's affairs began soon after the tragedy of a stillborn child. No coincidence either that according to recent statistics, the likeliest time for a man to have an affair is when his wife is pregnant. This is when a man is fearing the responsibilities of parenting, when he's afraid of settling into adulthood. It's the time, too, when his wife is turning toward a new love object—the child that's daily growing inside her. As a result, many men feel estranged from their wives during pregnancy, and instead of just talking to their wives about this emotional distance, they turn to extramarital affairs.

If a man, then, doesn't see his affair as somehow being symptomatic of the condition his marriage is in, if he doesn't see that his extramarital relationships reflect, at least in some way, on the state of his marriage, his marriage is headed for problems.

*     *     *

Lying about an affair, of course, is common. For many people, it's second nature, a habit learned early in life: In order for a relationship to work, in order for two human beings to live together at all harmoniously, there are just some things better left unsaid. If we were to be honest, if we were to really tell our spouses just what we thought and felt, then our marriages, many of us are convinced, would explode.

That belief is something a lot of us bring to our love relationships, again, the result of our earliest familial and societal conditioning. Lying, at least *white* lying, we feel, is an acceptable, even a necessary, survival skill, especially in a marriage.

And yet, paradoxically, all of us want to be able to trust our marriages. We want our love relationships to be the one place where we can truly be ourselves. But how can a trust and an openness develop between two people if lying is a built-in component?

The answer is simple. They can't. . . . If we tell a lie or if we conceal a truth from our mate, we're only creating more distance and less trust. And the more secrets we have from one another, the less intimacy exists in our relationship, and the more separate we feel from each other.

Still, so many of us try to justify our secrets, convincing ourselves that what we're really doing by lying is protecting our mates (and not ourselves) from unnecessary pain. But again—and it's something we all know but something we conveniently forget—we only end up compounding our own pain and our mate's pain by telling a lie or concealing a truth. Dr. Don Jackson, the well-known family therapist, underscores this point: "You must overcome your fear of honesty, because every lie begets another lie. It is always necessary to cover the cover-up."

Besides, our attempts at deception are likely to be unsuccessful anyway. If we're trying to keep a lie from the person we're supposedly closest with in the world, we can't help but be guarded and unspontaneous. And if our spouses, after all, can't pick up on these sorts of shifts in our behavior, who can? We're often, therefore, not *keeping* a lie from our spouses. We're simply *colluding* with them to keep a painful bit of information out of awareness.

So should a man tell the truth to his wife if he's having, or if he's had, an affair? Or is it enough for him just to know that any affair he's having is a reflection on the emotional well-being of his marriage? Well, if he's interested in maintaining a trusting relationship, being honest is his only alternative. If he's interested, too, in feeling close and uninhibited with the woman he's presumably going to be spending the rest of his life with, honesty, again, is necessary: In a marriage, lies simply have a way of clogging up love's passageways.

Honesty creates trust, and trust creates love. If we can be honest in our marriages, we can create trusting and loving relationships. And loving relationships rarely succumb to the Lust Demon. If a husband and a wife, therefore, can confide their attractions for other people to each other and not have to hide them, they'll ultimately have a much easier time dealing with this Lust Demon. Sharing sexual attractions, moreover, tends to dissipate their allure. What's no longer forbidden often stops being so seductive.

Being honest in a relationship, then, is the preventive for the Lust Demon. Being honest in a relationship, however, means more than simply confessing to an adultery or an attraction. It means, ultimately, being able to share with your mate, as gently as possible, your deepest haunts about the love you're feeling for them, as well as the deepest self-doubts you're feeling about yourself. If a couple can manage that, though, and if they can be wise enough to receive each other's honesty without overreacting, love will usually do the rest.

\* \* \*

Extramarital sex is a very volatile subject for any couple. This is because the deepest layers of our emotional lives are inextricably bound to the sexual relationships we have with our spouses. "There is a deep association," Nena O'Neill says, "between sex as a physical act of closeness and our feelings of attachment and affection. As infants," she elaborates, "we are held and caressed, soothed and cuddled by our parents, and thus learn to associate physical closeness with love and security. . . . Given this and our internalization of traditional expectations for sex with only one person, sexual fidelity is not just a vow in marriage or a moral or religious belief, but a need associated with our deepest emotions and our quest for emotional security."

Like it or not, the majority of us need sexual fidelity in our marriages. It's part of a more primal emotional loyalty that all of us require.

The Lust Demon, by jeopardizing our most enduring and emotionally supportive relationships, threatens our most basic needs. And when these basic needs are threatened, the resulting pain can be unbearable.

\* \* \*

The Lust Demon never totally disappears from a marriage. It swims, either dormantly or else much closer to the surface, within both partners. But again, there *is* a preventive for the potential damages it can wreak. Namely, by befriending the Lust Demon with honesty, it can be tamed. It doesn't necessarily have to be, as it so often is, therefore, either the cause or the excuse for wrecking a marriage. But that sort of honesty demands a degree of bravery and trust that too many of us too easily dismiss as unrealistic.

# CHAPTER SEVEN
# CONCLUSIONS

I N THIS BOOK, I've attempted to briefly explore some of the emotional demons of romantic relationships. Every such relationship, as I pointed out—to varying degrees of intensity and to varying degrees of awareness—necessarily traverses the six terrains I outlined. Every couple, in other words, at some point in their lives, must grapple with the issues of dependency, autonomy, anger, jealousy, infidelity, and the complex logistics of finding time to be together.

I tried to make clear that many relationships become either stuck or unglued at one or a combination of these emotional obstacles. Some couples, for example, play out—for a *lifetime*—their autonomy/dependency battles. Other couples capsize or else angrily tread water in the turbulent currents of the Jealousy Demon. Still other relationships succumb to a knotty combination of all these demons.

What's hopefully clear by now is that if lovers don't attain some genuine resolution, some genuine reconciliation with each of these very difficult issues, then they'll probably have to battle them, either covertly or overtly, for the rest of their lives. But if a couple can wrestle with and come to some acceptable terms with these often painful issues, then they'll become stronger and more loving marital partners: Couples who make this journey, perforce, become more self-aware, more truthful, and more compassionate. These are, simply, the qualities that are needed, as well as created, along this journey.

What exactly is at the journey's end? I can't, unfortunately, promise anyone total fulfillment or utter marital bliss. I can't even promise an end to the journey. These demons just have a way of reappearing when long ago we thought them slain. What I can promise, though, and it's a major accomplishment in light of how few exist, is a relatively solid relationship filled with more moments of love.

In the end, we don't really have a choice whether or not to start on this journey. We're all thrust onto it the moment we meet someone we feel special about. These obstacles simply make themselves known to us in the course of any long-term relationship. Where we do have some real choice, though, is in how we choose to confront them.

Wrestling with these demons is, of course, hard work; and the majority of us, brought up in a society that trivializes marriage, just aren't motivated to do it. But what are the alternatives? To live without love? To avoid all intense relationships? To cultivate friendships that are satisfying but never substitutes for romantic involvements? Or worse, to tolerate mutually self-destructive relationships?

\*     \*     \*

As I pointed out, our culture, but especially its men, understand very little about emotional intimacy. What it does understand is sexual intimacy. Indeed, there has never been a society in the history of the world that's been so explicit and so preoccupied with the dance of sexual mating. It's almost as if we've all become fixated at these first stages of a love relationship.

Scoring, getting women into bed, having people sexu-ally fantasizing about us . . . it's as if *that* were the end point, as if sleeping with someone were the pot of gold at the rainbow's end. Maybe for a young adolescent male or female, that's appropriately an endpoint. But when it's still the exclusive pot of gold for a man, say in his late twenties or early thirties (as it was for many of the men I interviewed), well, then things are getting a bit out of hand.

The "real" gold, I've tried to stress, can be a lot more than the formation of a sexual connection. It can be the formation of an intimate and emotionally meaningful one. But again, a common practice in our day, as the well-known psychologist Rollo May points out, "is to avoid working up the courage required for authentic intimacy by shifting the issue to the body, making it a matter of simple physical courage. It is easier in our society," May says, "to be naked physically than to be naked psychologically or spiritually, easier to share our body than to share our fantasies, hopes, fears, and aspi-rations, which are felt to be more personal and the shar-ing of which is experienced as making us more vulnera-ble. For curious reasons," Dr. May adds, "we are shy about sharing the things that matter most."

We've become fixated at the body levels of intimacy—at sexual conquests and sexual performance—because the next levels of the dance of intimacy are just too frightening for most of us. These levels, with their inner demons, are, many feel, better left unexplored.

It's clearly very difficult to get people, but especially men, with their ofttimes monomaniacal careerist ambi-tions, to take a long and deep look at their relationships and at themselves. But again, just what are our alterna-

tives? To live with someone we feel indifference or hatred for? To never speak about what's tormenting us?
Or to maintain safe but uninspiring romantic relationships?

Being embroiled in an unrelenting twenty-five-year
battle with a spouse, or constantly having to maneuver
to avoid one another, takes great skill and wherewithal:
As much, if not more effort than trying honestly to deal
with your problems.

\* \* \*

Why is it that so many of us rout our love relationships, these relationships that, more than any others,
begin with so much hope? How is it possible, in these
relationships that are supposed to bring our most loving
parts, that it is our most grotesque emotions that too
often are provoked?

It's possible, bottom line, because we don't know one
of life's secrets: That our romantic relationships are potentially our greatest opportunities.

Our romantic relationships, very briefly, are part of a
lifelong process of perfecting ourselves—a process we
either consciously respect and embrace or one we un-
consciously squander away. Dr. Robert Seidenberg, a
practicing psychiatrist and psychoanalyst, succinctly ex-
presses this view of marriage:

> Marriage offers the major opportunity for personal
> and mutual growth that life provides. Only in mar-
> riage is one likely to experience the day-in-day-out
> confrontation with oneself through another. Not only
> one's integrative capacity but one's sanity is constantly
> tested in trying to determine what is fair or not.
> The everyday give-and-take that a marriage in-

volves is the best testing ground for growth. It's a most precious opportunity for getting to know what and who one really is. How generous, how tolerant, how unselfish, how brilliant one really is. . . . A man cannot be truly mature until he has been confronted with, and deals with, and hopefully masters, the painful exigencies of living to which the marital state alone is heir.

It's in our romantic relationships, therefore, where there's hope for all of us. If we can "get it together" in these relationships, then we can get it together anywhere else, for these intimate relationships present us with the most profound and most intense confrontations any of us have with our darkest and lightest sides.

Just how gracefully or how brutally we negotiate these relationships is, in the end, determined by nothing less than the degree to which we've understood ourselves and our fellow human beings.

# BIBLIOGRAPHY

## BOOKS

Avendon, Burt. *Ah, Men!* New York: A & W Publishers, Inc., 1980.

Bach, George R. and Torbet, Laura. *A Time for Caring.* New York: Delacorte Press, 1982.

Bergman, Ingmar. *Scenes from a Marriage.* New York: Pantheon Books, Inc., 1974.

Berman, Steve and Weiss, Vivien. *Relationships.* New York: Hawthorn Books, Inc., 1978.

Bernard, Jessie. *The Future of Marriage.* New York: World Publishing Company, 1972.

Brain, Robert. *Friends and Lovers.* New York: Basic Books, Inc., 1976.

Callahan, Roger with Levine, Karen. *It Can Happen to You.* New York: A & W Publishers, Inc., 1982.

Castillejo, Irene de. *Knowing Woman.* New York: G. P. Putnam's Sons, 1973.

Davidson, Terry. *Conjugal Crime.* New York: Hawthorn Books, Inc., 1978.

Dinnerstein, Dorothy. *The Mermaid and the Minotaur.* New York: Harper & Row, 1977.

Friday, Nancy. *Men in Love.* New York: Delacorte Press, 1980.

Garbo, Norman. *To Love Again.* New York: McGraw-Hill Book Company, 1977.

Goldberg, Arnold. *The Psychology of the Self.* (Written with the collaboration of Heinz Kohut.) New York: International Universities Press, Inc., 1978.

Goldberg, Herb. *The Hazards of Being Male.* New York: Nash Publishing, 1976.

Heydt, Vera von der. *Fathers and Mothers.* ("On the Father in Psychotherapy".) Zurich: Spring Publications, 1973.

Horney, Karen. *Feminine Psychology*. New York: W. W. Norton & Company, Inc., 1973.

————. *Neurosis and Human Growth*. New York: W. W. Norton & Company, Inc., 1950.

Kaplan, Louise J. *Oneness & Separateness: From Infant to Individual*. New York: Simon & Schuster, 1978.

Keys, James. *Only Two Can Play This Game*. New York: The Julian Press, Inc., 1972.

Laing, R. D. *Self and Others*. Great Britain: Tavistock Publications, 1971.

Lasch, Christopher. *The Culture of Narcissism*. New York: W. W. Norton & Company, Inc., 1979.

Lazarre, Jane. *On Loving Men*. New York: The Dial Press, 1978.

Lederer, William J. and Jackson, Don D. *The Mirages of Marriage*. New York: W. W. Norton & Company, Inc., 1968.

Lee, John Alan. *The Colors of Love*. New Jersey: Prentice-Hall, Inc., 1976.

Leonard, Michael. *The Men's Club*. New York: Farrar, Strauss & Giroux, 1981.

Levinson, Daniel J. *The Seasons of a Man's Life*. New York: Alfred A. Knopf, Inc., 1978.

Mace, David and Mace, Vera. *Marriage East & West*. Garden City, New York: Dolphin Books/Doubleday & Company, Inc., 1959.

Mahler, Margaret S., Pine, Fred and Bergman, Anni. *The Psychological Birth of the Human Infant*. New York: Basic Books, Inc., 1975.

May, Rollo. *The Course to Create*. New York: W. W. Norton & Company, Inc., 1975.

Mayeroff, Milton. *On Caring*. New York: Harper & Row, Inc., 1971.

Menninger, Karl. *Love Against Hate*. New York: Harcourt, Brace & World, Inc., 1942.

Minuchin, Salvador. *Families & Family Therapy.* Cambridge, Massachusetts: Harvard University Press, 1974.

O'Neill, Nena. *The Marriage Premise.* New York: M. Evans and Company, Inc., 1977.

O'Neill, Nena and O'Neill, George. *Shifting Gears.* New York: M. Evans and Company, Inc., 1974.

Paolino, Thomas J. and McCrady, Barbara S. *Marriage & Marital Therapy.* New York: Brunner/Mazel, 1978.

Pietropinto, Anthony, and Simenauer, Jacqueline. *Husbands and Wives.* New York: Times Books, 1979.

Ravich, Robert A. and Wyden, Barbara. *Predictable Pairing.* New York: Peter H. Wyden, 1974.

Rogers, Carl R. *Becoming Partners: Marriage and Its Alternatives.* New York: Delacorte Press, 1972.

Sanford, John A. *The Invisible Partners.* New York: Paulist Press, 1980.

Scarf, Maggie. *Unfinished Business.* Garden City, New York: Doubleday & Company, Inc., 1980.

Seidenberg, Robert. *Marriage Between Equals.* New York: Anchor Press/Doubleday, 1973.

Shapiro, David. *Neurotic Styles.* New York: Basic Books, Inc., 1965.

Spangler, David. *Relationships & Identity.* Forres, Scotland: Findhorn Publications, 1978.

Tennov, Dorothy. *Love and Limerence.* New York: Stein and Day, 1979.

Thorp, Roderick and Blake, Robert. *Wives.* New York: M. Evans and Company, Inc., 1971.

Watzlawick, Paul, Weakland, John and Fisch, Richard. *Change.* New York: W. W. Norton & Company, Inc., 1974.

West, Uta. *If Love Is the Answer, What Is the Question?* New York: McGraw-Hill Book Company, 1977.

Wheelis, Allen. *On Not Knowing How to Live.* New York: Harper & Row, Publishers, Inc., 1975.

Williams, Juanita H. *Psychology of Women.* New York: W. W. Norton & Company, Inc., 1974.

**ARTICLES**

Carlson, Nancy L. "Male Client—Female Therapist." *The Personnel and Guidance Journal.* December, 1981:228–231.

Greenfield, Jeff. "Why Marriage on TV Has Become a Combat Zone." *TV Guide.* April 17–23, 1982:7–10.

Skovholt, Thomas M. and Morgan, James I. "Career Development: An Outline of Issues for Men." *The Personnel and Guidance Journal.* December, 1981:231–237.

# ABOUT THE AUTHOR

STEVE BERMAN is a psychiatric journalist, screenwriter, and psychotherapist whose books include *Relationships* and *What to Be*. His articles and essays about men and marriage appear in dozens of national magazines and newspapers. He lives with his wife, Vivien, and daughter, Jennarose, in Northampton, Massachusetts.

**Catalog**

If you are interested in a list of fine Paperback
books, covering a wide range of subjects
and interests, send your name and address,
requesting your free catalog, to:

McGraw-Hill Paperbacks
1221 Avenue of Americas
New York, N.Y. 10020